Stage 3 Paper 12

Business Taxation
(Finance Act 1998)

Fifth edition January 1999

ISBN 0 7517 3481 0 (previous edition 0 7517 3437 3)

British Library Cataloguing-in-Publication Data

A catalogue record for this book
is available from the British Library

Published by

BPP Publishing Limited
Aldine House, Aldine Place
London W12 8AW

http://www.bpp.co.uk

Printed in Great Britain by Ashford Colour Press, Gosport, Hants.

If you use CIMA **Passcards**, you can be sure that the time you spend on final revision for your **1999 exams** is time well spent.

- They **save you time**: following the structure of the BPP Study Text for Paper 12, important facts on key exam topics are summarised for you

- They incorporate diagrams to kick start your memory

- They are pocket-sized: you can run through them **anytime** and **anywhere**

CIMA **Passcards** focus on the exam you will be facing.

- They highlight which topics have been examined - and when

- They provide you with suggestions on subject examinability, given past exams and the direction the examiner appears to be taking, in **exam focus points**

- They give you useful **exam hints** that can earn you those vital extra marks in the exam

Run through the complete set of **Passcards** as often as you can during your final revision period. The day before the exam, try to go through the **Passcards** again. You will then be well on your way to passing your exams. **Good luck**

Page

Exam focus. In this chapter we will cover the structure of the personal tax computation. Although you will only have to prepare the simplest personal computations, always remember that an individual's affairs must be considered as a whole. This is especially important when you do any tax planning.

Administration

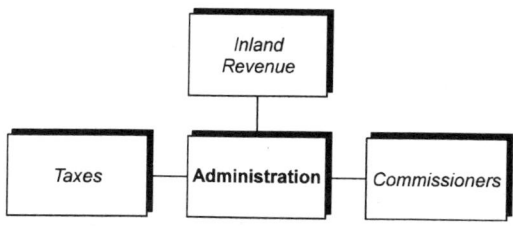

Taxes

The main *taxes* are as follows.

- Income tax

- Corporation tax

- Capital gains tax (CGT)

- Value added tax (VAT)

All of these taxes are administered by the Inland Revenue, apart from VAT which is administered by HM Customs & Excise.

The law is laid down in Acts of Parliament and in statutory instruments, and is interpreted in court decisions. The main amendments to the law each year are proposed in a Budget, and enacted in a Finance Act.

Most changes in the law relating to income tax take effect from the start of a tax year, because income tax is charged for tax years. The tax year 1998/99 runs from 6 April 1998 to 5 April 1999.

The Inland Revenue

Inspectors of Taxes examine the returns of individuals, businesses and companies. Collectors of taxes collect any tax due.

The Inland Revenue is gradually setting up three sorts of office:

- Taxpayer Service Offices to do routine checking, computation and collection work

- Taxpayer District Offices to investigate selected accounts, deal with corporation tax and enforce the payment of tax

- Taxpayer Assistance Offices to handle enquiries

Commissioners

If a taxpayer disagrees with a Revenue decision, he may appeal to the commissioners. There are two sorts of commissioner.

- General commissioners are unpaid lay people
- Special commissioners are paid experts

Further appeals may be made to the courts.

Computations

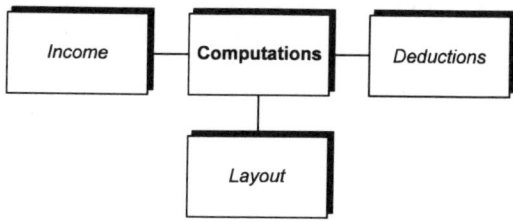

A basic principle of income tax is the *aggregation of income*. All of an individual's income for a tax year, from all sources, is added up in a personal tax computation. The result, minus charges, is *statutory total income (STI)*.

Income

- Income which is not taxed at source is taxed under the rules of a *schedule*. The schedules are as follows
  - Schedule A: rent from land and buildings
  - Schedule D
    - Case I: profits of trades
    - Case II: profits of professions and vocations
    - Case III: interest received gross
    - Case IV: income from foreign securities
    - Case V: income from other foreign possessions
    - Case VI: income not within any other schedule or case
  - Schedule E: income from employment

- Many sorts of investment income are *taxed at source*: for example for every £100 of bank interest income, the individual only receives £80. The taxable income is £100, but credit is given for the tax suffered o   This applies to dividends, to bank and building society interest, to interest on debentures and to patent royalties

---

Exam focus. You are most likely to have to think about investment income when you are advising on the net effect of an increase in trading or employment income: investment income may mean that the marginal rate of tax is 40%.

Deductions

- *Charges* on income are deducted from income to get to STI. The charges are as follows

  o   Covenanted payments to charity, where the covenant may last for more than three years

  o   One-off gifts to charity

  o   Payments of interest where the loan is used for a qualifying purpose, mainly buying into certain businesses

  o   Certain other payments for commercial purposes, including patent royalties

  o   Payments for vocational training

- The *personal allowance* is deducted from STI to get to taxable income

Layout

- You should total *non-savings income* and *savings income* separately. Deduct charges and the personal allowance from non-savings income first

- Once you have found the taxable income, treat savings income as the top slice of that income. Savings income falling in the basic rate band is then taxed at only 20%.

Savings income falling within the higher rate band is taxed at 40%

Exam focus. This special treatment of savings income is important when you are deciding whether to reward a director with salary or dividends: the income tax on dividends may be lower than on salary.

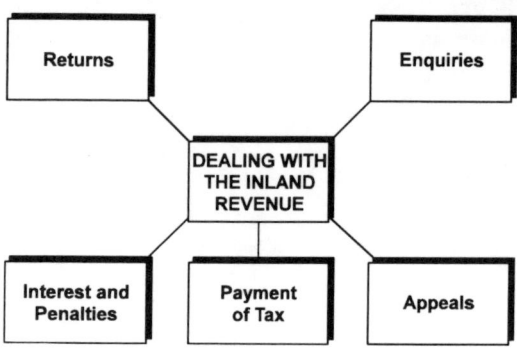

Returns   5/97

A *tax return* is made for each tax year.

- A taxpayer can calculate his own tax on the return. This calculation is a *self-assessment:* a tax demand which the taxpayer writes himself

- Income tax is due on 31 January following the tax year, with payments on account 12 months and 6 months earlier

Enquiries   5/97

The Revenue randomly select returns to enquire into. They also select returns where there is an identified tax risk.

Time limit

- Written notice of an enquiry must be given by a year after the later of

  o the filing date;

o the 31 January, 30 April, 31 July or 31 October next following the actual delivery date of the return or amendment to the return

Powers

- The Revenue can demand that taxpayers produce documents

- Documents relating to an appeal need not be produced and taxpayers can appeal against a demand for documents.

Payment of tax

- The normal payment dates for income tax and Class 4 NICs in a tax year are:
  - o 31 January in the tax year for the first payment on account (POA);
  - o 31 July following the tax year for the second POA; and
  - o 31 January following the tax year for the final payment.

Appeals

- A taxpayer may appeal against
  - o any assessment, except a self assessment
  - o an amendment to a self assessment or a disallowance of a claim or election, following an enquiry or discovery
  - o a demand for documents

- The *time limit* for an appeal is 30 days from the issue of the assessment, amendment, disallowance or demand

- The appeal may be settled by agreement. If not, the *hearing* is before the commissioners. Further appeal, on a point of law (not one of fact), lies to the courts

Interest and penalties   *5/97, 11/97*

- There is a fixed penalty and a daily penalty for failure to make a tax return

- There is a tax geared penalty of up to 100% of the tax which would have been lost for an incorrect return submitted fraudulently or negligently

- There is a fixed penalty and a daily penalty for failure to produce documents demanded

- Interest is charged on tax not paid by the due date

- Surcharges may also apply to tax not paid by specified dates.

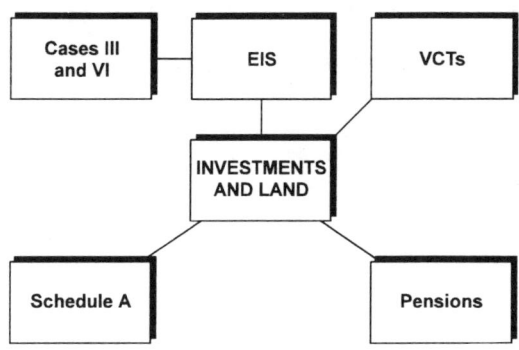

Cases III and VI

Schedule D Case III taxes interest received gross.

Schedule D Case VI covers income not falling under any other schedule or case.

EIS 5/95, 11/96

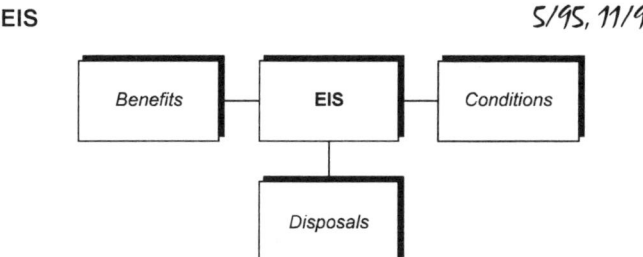

The new *EIS* (enterprise investment scheme) offers tax relief for capital invested in the ordinary shares of unquoted trading companies, but no relief for dividend income. Only shares subscribed for qualify, not shares bought secondhand.

Benefits

- Investments save income tax of 20% of the amount invested

- On disposals more than five years after issue of the shares, gains are exempt from CGT

Conditions

- The company must be unquoted and carrying on a qualifying trade

- The investor must not hold more than 30% of the company's capital, and he must not be an employee or a non-qualifying director

- An individual can only invest £150,000 a year under the EIS. Participation in the scheme is limited to companies with gross assets of less than £15 million before an investment and no more than £16 million after

Disposals

- On a disposal within five years of issue of the shares, the tax reduction is withdrawn
  - The withdrawal on an arm's length sale may be only partial

- On a later disposal, the tax reduction is not withdrawn and any gain is exempt from CGT
  - The CGT exemption is limited if EIS relief has been partly withdrawn, and is zero if it has all been withdrawn

VCTs

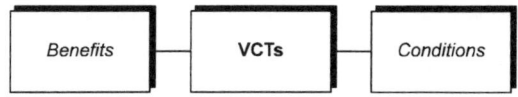

VCTs (venture capital trusts) are quoted investment trusts which buy shares in unquoted trading companies.

Benefits

Individual investors in VCTs obtain the following benefits on the first £100,000 invested each tax year.

- An income tax reduction of 20% of the amount invested, so long as the shares are subscribed for

- Tax-free dividends and capital gains, whether the shares are subscribed for or bought secondhand

Conditions

- The VCT must have at least 70% of its investments in *qualifying holdings*, and at least 30% of those qualifying holdings must be *eligible shares*

- The tax reduction on issue is wholly or partly withdrawn on a disposal within five years

Exam focus. Make sure that you can explain the difference between the EIS and VCTs: the EIS is for direct investment in unquoted companies, whereas VCTs are for indirect investment, and carry an extra privilege - tax-free dividends.

Pensions   5/95

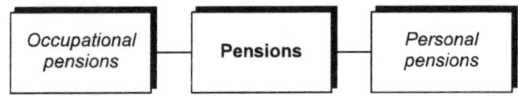

Occupational pensions

Employers can set up approved schemes which they contribute to, and which their employees may contribute to. The advantages are as follows.

- Contributions by both employers and employees are tax-deductible

- The fund pays no tax on its income or gains

- On retirement, the employee may take a tax-free lump sum as well as a (taxable) pension

Schemes are subject to limits as follows.

- The employee's contributions are limited to 15% of gross emoluments

- The maximum lump sum is final remuneration × 1.5

- The maximum pension is final remuneration × 2/3

- For all of the above limits, earnings above the earnings cap are ignored

---

Exam focus. The examiner is now concentrating on employees more than he used to, and a pension scheme is a very important benefit for many employees.

Personal pensions

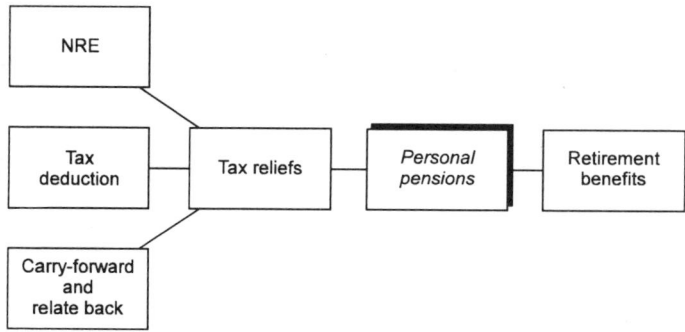

Tax reliefs

- Tax reliefs are as follows

    - Contributions are tax-deductible

    - The limit on contributions is a percentage of *NRE* (net relevant earnings). The percentage varies with age. NRE is earnings minus schedule E deductions and excess trade charges. The earnings cap applies to NRE

    - *Carry-forward* of relief is allowed, for up to six years

    - A taxpayer can *relate back* premiums to the tax year before the year of payment

- *Retirement benefits* may be taken at any age between 50 and 75. Up to 25% of the value of the fund may be taken as a tax-free lump sum. The rest of the fund must be used to buy an annuity. Income withdrawals are allowed before an annuity is bought

Schedule A

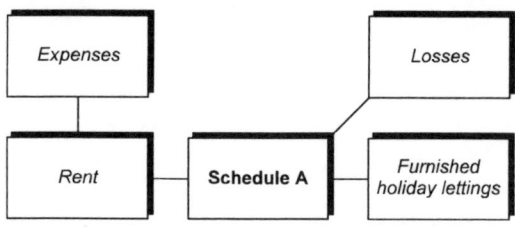

Schedule A covers rent from property in the UK. A landlord has a single Schedule A business, and accounts are drawn up just as for a trader (but with a year-end of 5 April).

- *Rent* is taxable on an accruals basis
  - If a lease for n years (under 50) is granted for a premium, the proportion of the premium treated as rent is $[1 - 0.02(n - 1)]$

- *Expenses* are as for a trader, including capital allowances (not given on plant or machinery let for use in a dwelling)

- Carry forward *losses* against future Schedule A income

Furnished holiday lettings are treated as trades for many income tax and CGT purposes. Keep a Schedule A business profit and loss account for all furnished holiday lettings, separate from the account for other lettings.

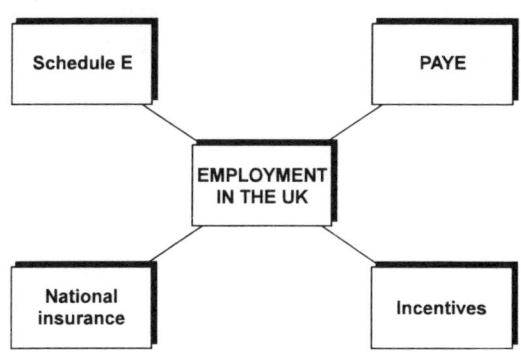

Schedule E   5/95, 5/96, 11/97

Schedule E applies to income from employment, the most common form of income. It applies to pay, taxable benefits and other income (for example tips).

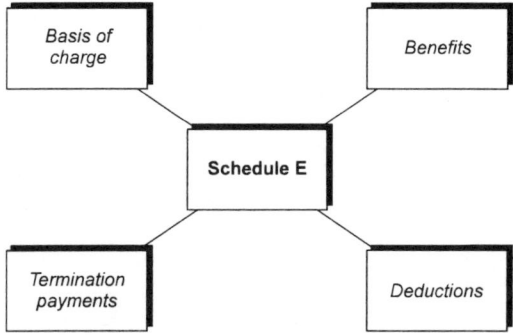

Basis of charge

Earnings are taxed in the year in which they are received. This means the actual date of payment or the time entitlement to payment arises, whichever comes first. Directors are deemed to receive earnings on the earliest of the following.

- The time given by the general rule

- The time the amount is credited in the company's accounting records

- The end of the company's period of account (if the amount has been determined by then)

- When the amount is determined, if this is after the end of the company's period of account

Schedule E only applies to employees, not to the self-employed. An employee works under a contract of service and a self-employed person under a contract for services.

Benefits (everyone)   *5/96, 11/96, 5/97*

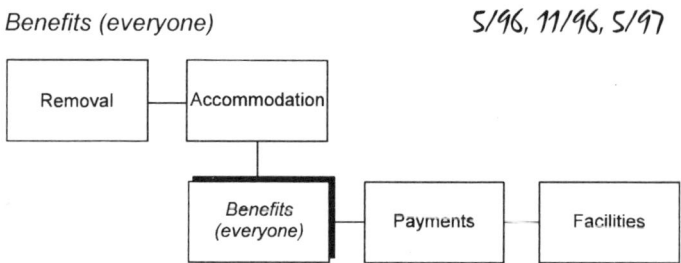

Benefits are generally taxable at their (marginal) cost to the employer. However, for employees earning less than £8,500 a year we take what the employee could sell them for. The following benefits are taxable under special rules.

- The annual value of *accommodation* is a taxable benefit, unless the accommodation is job-related. If the cost of the property was more than £75,000, there is an extra charge of the excess × the official rate of interest at the start of the year

- When an employee has to move house because of his job, and his employer pays *removal* expenses, the first £8,000 of the payment is not a taxable benefit

- Payments to employees are treated as follows
  - The cost of vouchers and the amount spent using a credit token is taxable
  - Awards under suggestion schemes are taxable unless they are small and made under a formal scheme
  - Long service awards are only non-taxable if service is at least 20 years and the cost does not exceed £20 per year
  - Mileage payments for the use of the employee's own car on business are not taxable, up to the limit laid down in the fixed profit car scheme
  - Payments under scholarship and apprenticeship schemes may be tax-free if they are not greater than £7,000 a year

- Facilities for employees are treated as follows
  - Entertainment provided by third parties is not taxable
  - Sports facilities and workplace nurseries are not taxable

Benefits (higher-paid)   *5/96, 11/96, 11/97, 11/98*

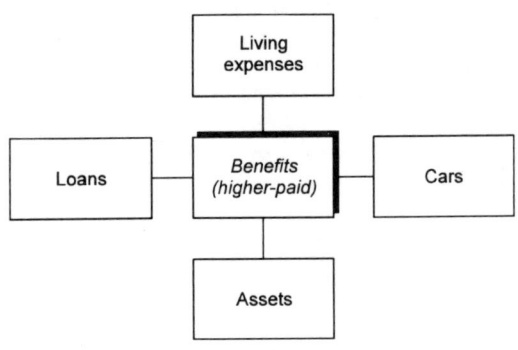

- *Living expenses* connected with accommodation, such as gas bills and redecoration, are taxable. If the accommodation is job-related, the maximum amount taxable is 10% of net emoluments

- The annual taxable benefit for the private use of a *car* is:

  (Price of car – capital contributions) × 35% × age factor × mileage factor

  o The age factor is 2/3 if the car is at least four years old at the end of the tax year; otherwise it is 1

  o The mileage factor is 1 for business mileage below 2,500. It is 2/3 for business mileage below 18,000, and 1/3 for business mileage of at least 18,000

  o The benefit and the mileage limits are scaled down on a time basis. The benefit is then reduced by any contribution by the employee for private use

  o Fuel is charged on a set scale, with no reduction for partial reimbursement by the employee

- If an *asset* other than a car or a mobile telephone is made available for private use, the annual taxable benefit is 20% of the market value when the asset was first provided, less any contribution by the employee. If an asset is later given or sold to the employee, the benefit is based on the original value less amounts already taxed, if that will give a higher value than the market value at the time of sale

  o There is a fixed benefit of £200 a year for mobile telephones

- *Loans* of over £5,000 give rise to taxable benefits, equal to the difference between the actual interest and interest at the official rate

  o A write-off of any loan gives rise to a taxable benefit equal to the amount written off

Deductions 5/97

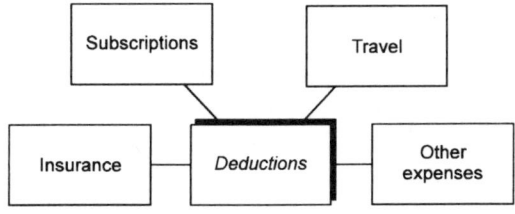

- *Insurance* premiums to cover directors' and employees' liabilities (and payments to meet those liabilities) are deductible

- *Subscriptions* to relevant professional bodies are deductible from Schedule E income

  . *Qualifying travel expenses* – full costs that the employee is obliged to incur in travelling in the performance of their duties or travelling to or from a place which they have to attend in the performance of duties. Normal commuting does not qualify.

- *Relief* is available for expenses incurred by an employee working at a temporary location on a secondment of 24 months or less.

- *Other expenses* are only deductible if they are incurred wholly, exclusively and necessarily in the performance of the duties of the employment. The strictness of this test has been emphasised in many cases

---

Exam focus. If you have to decide whether an expense is deductible, put yourself in the Revenue's position and try to find an argument against deducting it. If you can find a specific argument, the expense is probably not deductible.

Termination payments

If an employee has a contractual entitlement to a termination payment, it is taxable in full.

Ex gratia payments and statutory redundancy pay are taxable, but subject to an exemption for the first £30,000.

PAYE   *11/97*

The PAYE system collects tax from employees each payday, with the intention that over a tax year, the right total of tax will be collected. The routine each payday is as follows.

- Add the gross pay to the running total of gross pay for the tax year

- Use the employee's PAYE code to work out the amount of cumulative gross pay which is tax free

- Compute tax on the balance

- Deduct the tax already paid. The difference is the tax to deduct on this payday

The employer must pay over the tax deducted up to the 5th of each month by the 19th of the month. (Quarterly payment is allowed if the average monthly total of tax and NICs is less than £600.)

The year-end return must be submitted by 19 May. If it is not, penalties are imposed.

Incentives   *11/95*

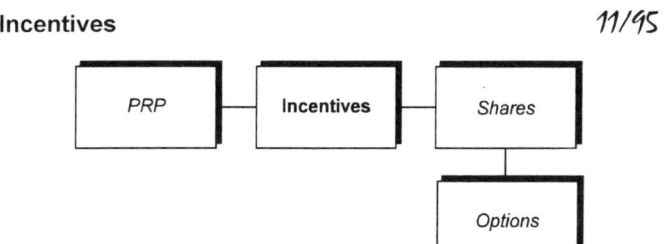

PRP

If an element of an employee's pay varies with the profits of his employment unit, under a scheme approved by the Inland Revenue, that element is exempt from income tax. For accounting periods beginning after 31.12.97 exempt income is limited to the lower of:

- 20% of total pay

- £2,000 a year

Thereafter, tax relief for PRP is to be phased out. The £2,000 ceiling is to be reduced to £1,000 from 1.1.99 and to £nil from 1.1.2000.

A PRP scheme cannot be restricted to only a select few employees.

The amount to share among employees must be either:

- A fixed percentage of profits, or

- A percentage of the amount shared out in the previous year, based on the change in profits from that year to the current year

Shares

There is a general charge to tax when a director or employee receives shares, of their market value minus the amount paid for them. This charge also applies when an option is exercised.

- Under a *profit sharing scheme*, a trust acquires shares and allocates them to employees. If the shares are not sold within five years from allocation, no Schedule E charge arises. Any gain on their eventual sale is, however, subject to CGT

  o The value of shares allocated to an employee in a tax year must not exceed £8,000. It must also not exceed the higher of £3,000 and 10% of the employee's salary

- Under an employee share ownership plan *(ESOP)*, a trust acquires shares and distributes them to employees

Options   *11/98*

- Under a *savings related share option scheme*, employees make regular monthly savings. The savings may be used to buy shares under options granted when the savings started. The only tax charge is to CGT on the disposal of the shares

- A company can set up a *company share option plan,* which may be restricted to a select few employees, as follows

  o Options may be issued to one employee covering shares up to a value of £30,000

  o Options must be exercised between three and ten years after grant, and once options have been exercised, the employee must wait three years before exercising any more options

  o The only tax charge is to CGT on the disposal of the shares

National insurance   *11/97, 5/98*

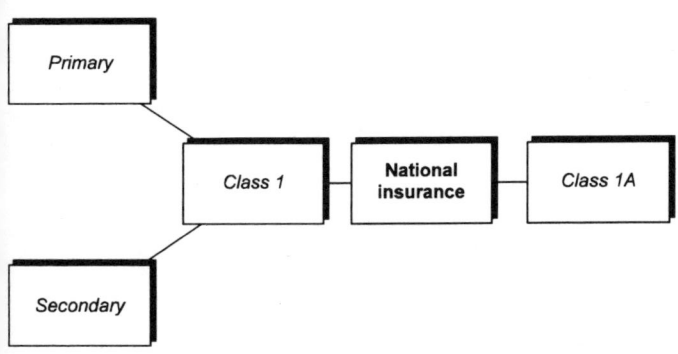

Class 1 primary

Employees pay primary contributions on their earnings, excluding most benefits in kind. Earnings are not reduced by expenses or pension contributions.

There are no contributions on earnings above the upper limit.

Class 1 secondary

Employers pay secondary contributions on their employees' earnings, with no upper limit.

Class 1A

Employers pay class 1A contributions on the taxable benefits of cars and fuel provided for private use by their employees.

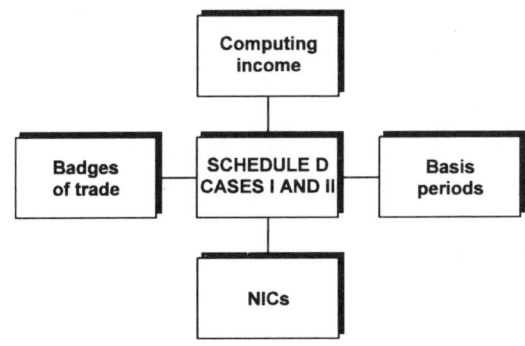

Badges of trade

The badges of trade are used to decide whether an individual is trading and therefore taxable under Schedule D Case I.

Computing income   *11/95, 5/97, 11/98*

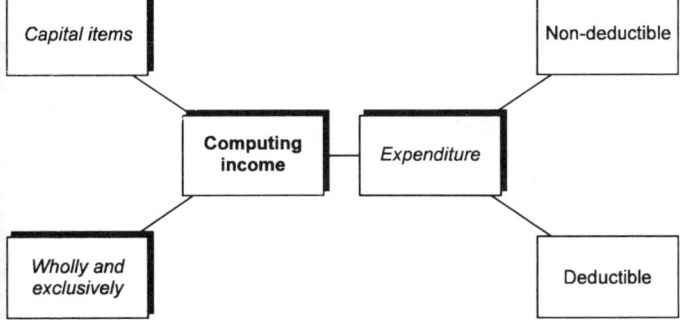

A trader's accounts profit (calculated on a 'true and fair basis') needs to be adjusted to arrive at his taxable profit. Some items of expenditure must be added back, and some items of income left out.

Capital items

Capital expenditure is not deductible.

- Repairs expenditure is deductible

    o Repairs to a newly-acquired asset may be capital (*Law Shipping*) or revenue (*Odeon Associated Theatres*)

Wholly and exclusively

Expenditure is only deductible if it was incurred wholly and exclusively for the purposes of the trade.

Non-deductible expenditure

Non-deductible items include the following

- Entertaining (except staff)
- Depreciation
- General provisions for doubtful debts

Deductible expenditure

Deductible items include the following.

- Small donations to local charities
- Interest
- Redundancy pay for staff (excess over statutory amount limited to 3 × statutory amount if trade ceases)
- Capital allowances
- Pre-trading expenditure

Basis periods   *5/96, 11/96, 11/97, 5/98, 11/98*

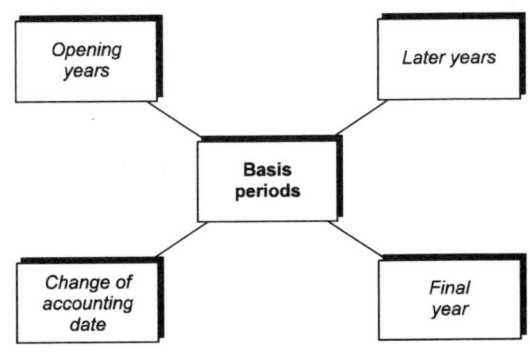

Opening years

The basis period for the first tax year runs from commencement to 5 April.

The basis period for the second tax year is as follows.

● If the accounting date in that year is at least 12 months from commencement, the 12 months to that date

● If the accounting date in that year is less than 12 months from commencement, the first 12 months

● If there is no accounting date in that year, the year itself

The basis period for the third tax year is the 12 months to the accounting date in that year.

Any profits taxed twice are *overlap profits.* They are deducted on changes of accounting date or on cessation.

Later years

The basis period for each tax year is the period of account ending in the year.

Final year   *5/98, 11/98*

The basis period for the final year starts at the end of the basis period for the previous year, and ends at cessation.

Any overlap profits not already deducted come off the final year's profits.

Change of accounting date

When a change of accounting date results in

- one short period of account ending in a tax year, the basis period for that year is always the 12 months to the new accounting date

- one long period of account ending in a tax year, the basis period for that year begins immediately after the end of the basis period for the previous year and ends on the new accounting date

- two periods of account ending in a tax year, the basis period for the year ends on the new accounting date. It begins immediately following the previous basis period

- no period of account ending in a tax year the basis period is the twelve months to the date that will be the new permanent accounting date

Overlap profits can be relieved on a change of accounting date if more than 12 months worth of profits would otherwise be taxed in a year

> *Exam focus.* You can easily check any computation which stretches over the whole life of a new business. The total taxable profits (less losses) should equal the total actual profits (less actual losses).

NICs

11/97, 5/98

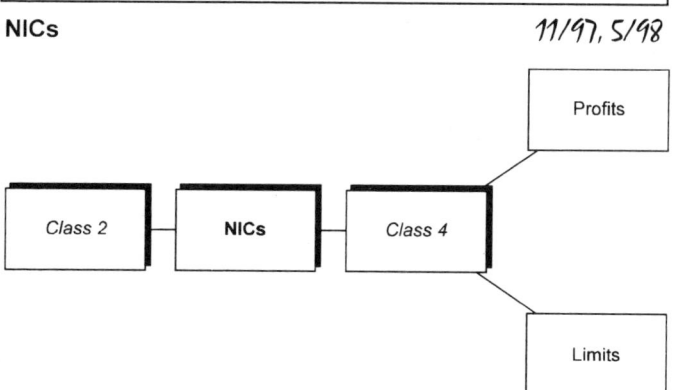

Class 2

The self employed pay class 2 NICs at a flat rate per week, unless profits are below the small earnings exemption.

Class 4

They also pay class 4 NICs, at 6% of their profits between the lower and upper *limits*.

- *Profits* are the taxable profits, as reduced by trade charges. Personal pension premiums do not reduce profits.

> *Exam focus.* In questions which ask whether someone should trade as a sole trader or through a company, the cost of NICs often tips the balance in favour of being a sole trader.

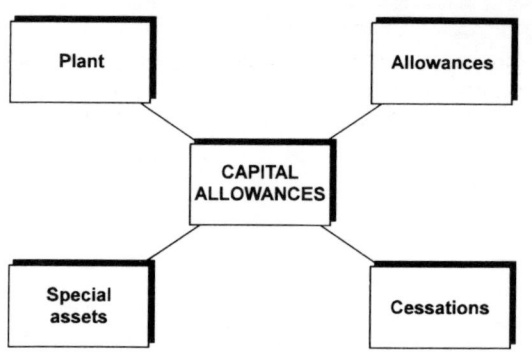

Capital allowances are given instead of depreciation, but they are only available for certain classes of asset. They are a trading expense.

Plant   5/96

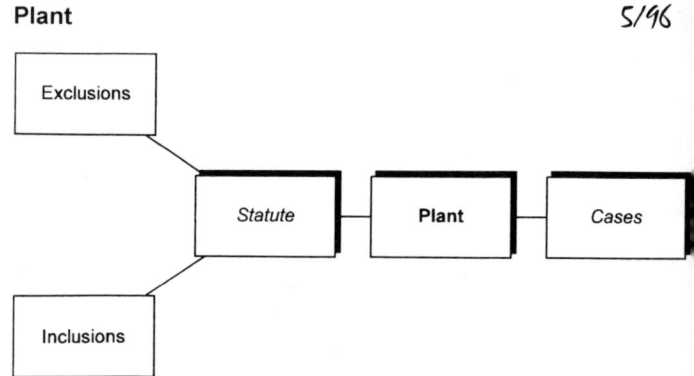

Statute: exclusions

The following items are excluded from being plant by statute.

- Buildings and parts of buildings
  - However, utility systems provided to meet the particular requirements of the trade, lifts, alarm systems and several other items can be plant

- Structures, with some exceptions such as dry docks and pipelines

- Land

Statute: inclusions

The following items qualify as plant by statute.

- Items needed to comply with fire regulations, thermal insulation and (for individuals) security assets

- Computer software

Cases

The courts tend to allow items as plant if they perform a function in the particular trade, rather than form part of the setting within which the trade is carried on. Thus a swimming pool, movable office partitions and special display lighting have been allowed, but not false ceilings, attractive floors and general lighting.

Allowances   *5/96, 11/96, 11/97, 5/98, 11/98*

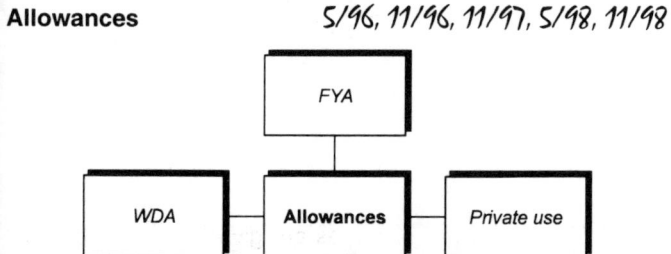

- The *WDA* (writing down allowance) is 25% × months/12, on the reducing balance basis. A reduced claim may be made, increasing the pool balance carried forward

- The WDA is 6% per annum on a reducing balance basis for certain assets (long life assets) with an expected working life of 25 years or more. These assets must be kept in their own pool

- Cars are pooled separately from other assets. Cars costing over £12,000 are kept in individual columns, with a maximum WDA of £3,000 per car per year

- An FYA (first year allowance) at double the normal WDA rate (ie 50% or 12%) is given on expenditure by certain businesses during the year to 1 July 1998. FYAs are not given on cars or leased assets

- For expenditure in the year to 1 July 1999 there is a FYA of 40% (not available to cars, leased assets or long life assets) for certain businesses

- The certain businesses qualifying for the above FYAs are small or medium sized sole traders or companies (turnover/assets/employees not exceeding £11.2 million/£5.6 million/250)

- If there is *private use* of an asset by a proprietor (not by an employee), the asset is kept outside the pool. The full value of the asset is shown in the computation, but only the business use proportion of the allowances may be claimed

Cessations   *5/98, 11/98*

Balancing adjustments

Balancing allowances or charges are given instead of WDAs on cessation, so as to deal with any remaining balances (after taking account of disposal proceeds). Balancing adjustments can also arise before cessation, whenever a column's balance becomes negative (charge) and whenever an asset which is not pooled with other assets is sold (allowance or charge).

Successions

When a business is transferred between connected persons, they may elect to transfer assets at their tax written down values, thus avoiding balancing adjustments.

Special assets

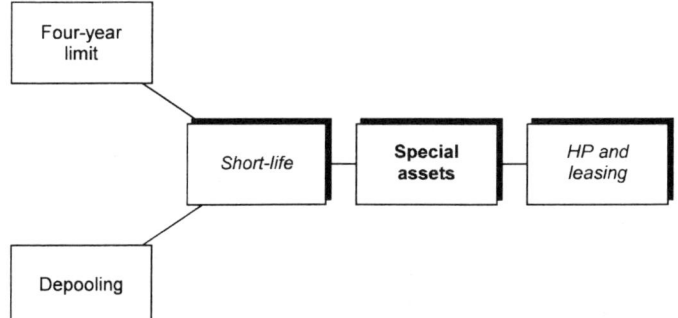

Short-life assets   5/98

Assets (but not cars or long life assets) may be *depooled*. They are then kept in their individual columns. There is a *four-year limit:* after this time, if the asset has not been disposed of, it is transferred to the pool.

HP and leasing

- If an asset is bought on HP, it is treated as bought outright for the cash price

- If an asset is leased, the rental payments are normally revenue expenditure. The lessor is the one who claims capital allowances

- If a car which would have cost more than £12,000 to buy is leased instead, only a proportion of each lease payment is deductible

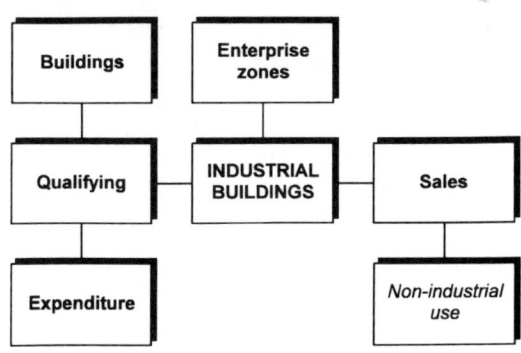

Qualifying buildings

- Factories and many warehouses qualify for industrial buildings allowances. Staff welfare buildings also qualify if the trade is qualifying

- Hotels can qualify

- Commercial buildings in enterprise zones qualify

Qualifying expenditure   *11/95, 11/97, 11/98*

The cost of a building and the cost of preparing the land qualify, but not the cost of the land itself.

If the cost of a non-industrial part of a building is 25% or less of the total cost, the total cost qualifies.

The allowance is a 4% straight-line writing down allowance.

Enterprise zones   *11/95*

For buildings in enterprise zones, there is a 100% initial allowance. Any amount not claimed is allowed on a straight-line basis, at 25% of the full cost each year.

Sales   *11/98*

There are industrial buildings allowances consequences on the sale of a building only if it is sold within its tax life.

- If a building has always been in industrial use, the balancing adjustment on sale is the difference between proceeds (limited to cost) and the residue before sale (the tax written down value)
  - o The buyer gets allowances of the residue after sale (the residue before sale plus the balancing charge/minus the balancing allowance), spread over the remaining tax life

- If there has been *non-industrial use* and a building is sold for more than original cost, the balancing charge is the actual allowances given. The residue after sale is the original cost minus the notional allowances

- If there has been *non-industrial use* and the building is sold for less than original cost, the balancing adjustment is the difference between the adjusted net cost and the actual allowances given. The residue after sale is the original cost, minus actual and notional allowances, plus the balancing charge/minus the balancing allowance

---

Exam focus. You may well be asked about buying secondhand buildings. Remember that a short remaining tax life means that the allowances will come in quickly. However also note that a building over 25 years old has no tax life left and hence is ineligible for allowances.

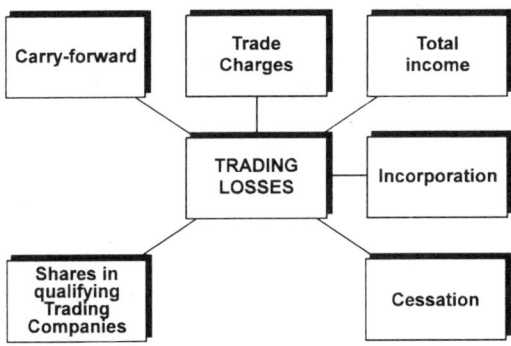

There is no general rule that sole traders can get relief for their losses. The conditions of a specific relief must be complied with.

Carry-forward (s 385)

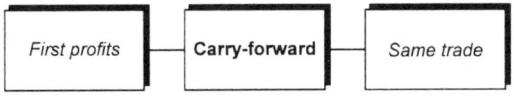

Losses not otherwise relieved are carried forward for relief against the *first profits* of the *same trade*. They cannot be saved up until it suits the trader to use them, and if the trade changes there is no relief.

Trade charges

If trade *charges* reduce STI to zero and some charges therefore go unrelieved, the unrelieved charges may be carried forward like a trading loss (s 387).

Total income (s 380)

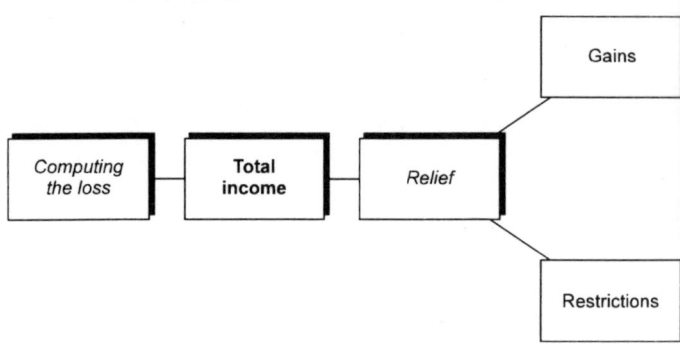

Computing the loss

- If a DI calculation gives a negative figure then DI for that tax year is NIL and instead a loss is available for relief.

Relief

Relief is against the STI of the tax year of the loss and/or the preceding tax year.

Gains

Once the income for a tax year has been fully covered, the taxpayer may choose to extend the claim to chargeable gains of the same year, less capital losses of the same year and brought forward.

Restrictions

- Relief under s 380 is not available unless the trade is on a commercial basis with a view to the realisation of profit

- Partial claims are not allowed: the whole loss must be set off, so far as there is income (or, if chosen, gains) available to absorb it in the chosen tax year of relief

---

Exam focus. Before recommending s 380 relief, consider whether it would lead to the waste of the personal allowance. This is often a significant tax planning point.

Incorporation (s 386)

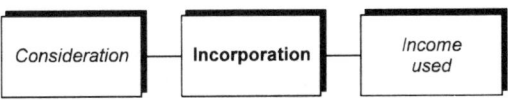

When a business is incorporated, pre-incorporation losses can be carried forward by the trader (not by the company) against income he receives from the company.

The *consideration* for the sale of the company must be wholly or mainly shares, and these shares must be retained throughout any tax year in which the loss is relieved.

The *income used* to absorb the loss is firstly salary and then dividends and interest received from the company.

Shares in qualifying trading companies (s 574)

Allowable capital losses incurred on shares subscribed for in unquoted trading companies may be deducted from the taxpayer's income in the year of the disposal and/or in the preceding year.

Cessation

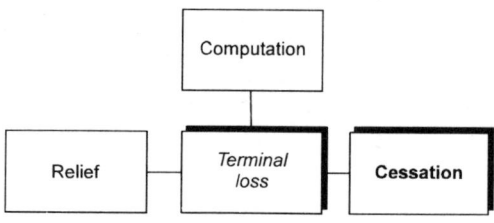

Terminal loss relief (s 388)

A loss in the last 12 months of trading can be set against the trading profits taxable in the tax year of cessation and in the preceding three years. Relief is given in later years first.

The *computation* of the loss involves taking the loss in the last tax year, plus the proportion of the loss in the preceding tax year corresponding to the period from 12 months before cessation to 5 April.

Any unrelieved overlap profits are added to the loss in the last year.

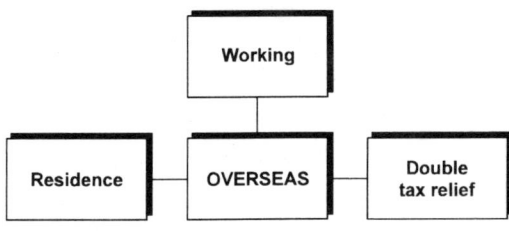

Residence

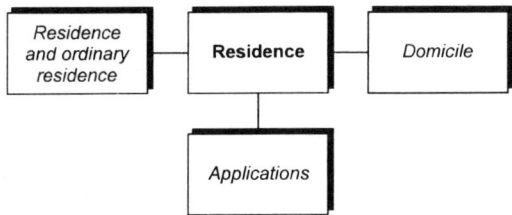

Residence and ordinary residence

An individual is resident in the UK for a tax year if he is in the UK for 183 days, or if he makes substantial annual visits to the UK.

An individual's *ordinary residence* is the country where he normally lives.

Domicile

An individual is domiciled in the country which is his permanent home. Someone can only change domicile by severing ties with the old country and establishing a permanent life in the new country.

Applications of the rules

- UK residents are taxable on worldwide income. Non-residents are taxable on UK income

- Non-UK domiciled UK residents are only taxable on overseas income if it is remitted to the UK or if it is Schedule E Case I income

Working

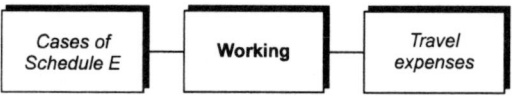

There are *three cases* of Schedule E. Case III income is only taxed if it is remitted to the UK.

Prior to 17 March 1998 there was a deduction available against overseas income taxed under Sch E Case I.

Travel expenses

- Expenses of travel to and from an overseas employment, and the cost of board and lodging outside the UK, are deductible.

- An employee working abroad for at least 60 days is not taxed on the cost of up to two return visits abroad by his family if the employer pays.

Double taxation relief

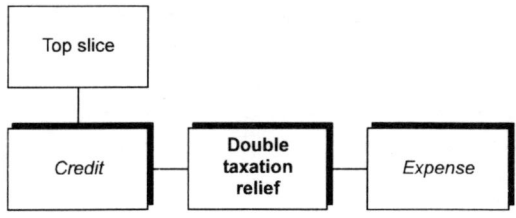

Credit relief

- Foreign income is brought into the tax computation gross and is treated as the *top slice* of an individual's income

  o If there is more than one source of foreign income, take as the top slice the income which has suffered foreign tax at the highest rate

- The relief, which is deducted from the UK tax, is the lower of the foreign tax and the UK tax on the foreign income

Expense relief

Foreign income is brought into the tax computation net of the foreign tax, and there is no deduction from the UK tax.

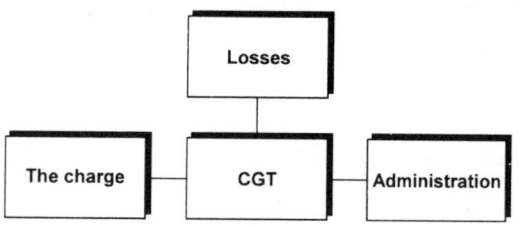

CGT was introduced in 1965. Since then the base date has been moved forward to 31 March 1982, so that only gains arising since then are taxed.

The charge

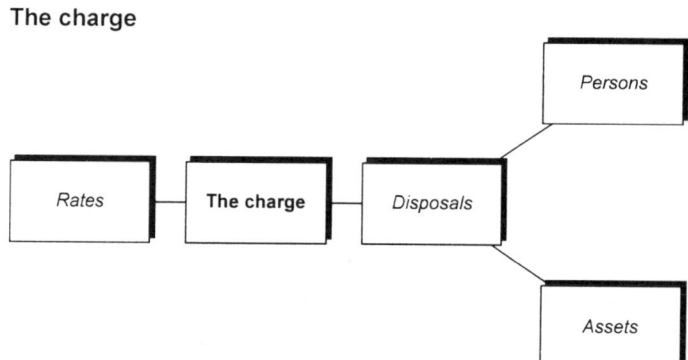

Rates

An individual has an annual CGT exemption. He or she then has *one* set of rate bands, allocated as follows.

- Lower rate: non-savings income, gains, savings income

- Basic rate: non-savings income, savings income, gains

Any remaining income and gains are taxed at 40%.

Disposals

Three elements are needed for CGT to arise.

- A *chargeable disposal:* this includes sales, gifts and the destruction of assets

- A *chargeable person:* individuals and companies are both chargeable, although companies pay corporation tax on their gains instead of CGT

- A *chargeable asset:* most assets are chargeable, but cars, some chattels and (for individuals) gilts and qualifying corporate bonds are exempt

---

Exam focus. Questions concentrate on business assets, but these can include investments and chattels (such as movable plant).

Losses

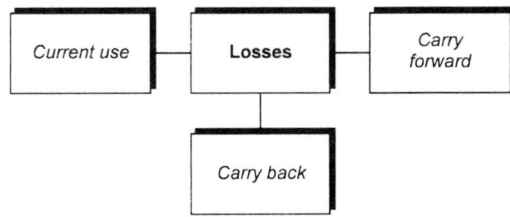

- *Current use:* start by setting losses in a tax year against gains in the same tax year, even if the gains are less than the annual exemption

- *Carry forward* unused losses against the first available net gains of future years. Only use losses brought forward to bring those net gains down to the annual exemption

- *Carry back* net losses in the year of death of an individual against net gains of the preceding three years, later years first. Only use losses brought back to bring those net gains down to the annual exemption

---

Exam focus. If you are dealing with a company, remember to work in accounting periods. Also remember that companies do not have an annual exemption and do not have a year of death from which to carry back losses (winding-up does not count).

Administration

The due date for CGT for an individual is 31 January following the tax year.

Where the consideration for a disposal is receivable in instalments over a period of more than 18 months, the CGT may be paid over the same period (up to a maximum of eight years) if paying it in one sum would cause undue hardship.

For companies (paying CT rather than CGT) the due date for tax is nine months after the end of the accounting period.

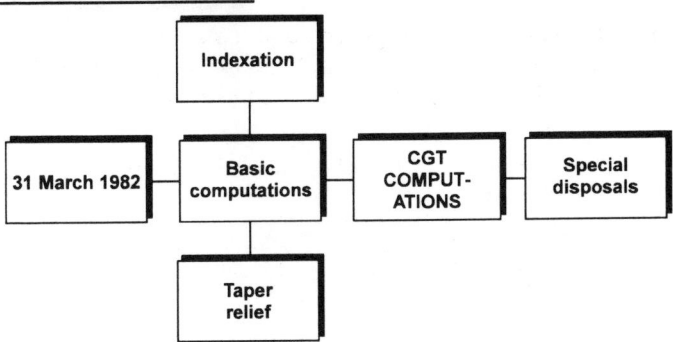

Gains are computed in a straightforward manner: proceeds – cost – indexation allowance. However, special rules are needed for some types of asset or disposal and taper relief is available on some disposals by individuals.

The basic CGT computation

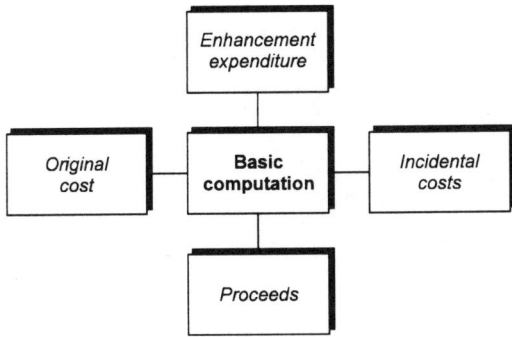

- The *original cost* of an asset to take into account is usually what was paid for it. Market value is used if it was used as proceeds for the person who sold the asset to the present owner

- Take *enhancement expenditure* into account if it is reflected in the state or nature of the asset at the time of disposal, or if it was on preserving the owner's legal right to the asset

- Take *incidental costs* of acquisition or disposal into account

- The *proceeds* are usually the actual proceeds, but they are increased to market value for gifts and for disposals which are not bargains at arm's length

Indexation

Give the indexation allowance, based on the RPI, so as not to tax gains due to inflation since March 1982. The CIMA examiner will give you the factors you need. For individuals indexation allowance is not calculated for periods after April 1998.

The indexation allowance can only reduce a gain as far as zero: it cannot create or increase a loss.

Taper relief

For gains realised by individuals after 5 April 1998 taper relief will reduce the amount of chargeable gain according to how long the asset has been owned for periods after 5 April 1998 and whether the asset is a business or non-business asset.

31 March 1982   *5/95, 11/95, 5/97, 11/98*

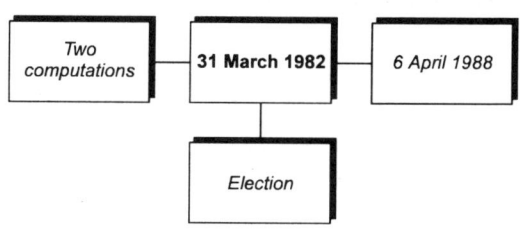

When an asset was owned on 31 March 1982, do *two computations*. The first one uses cost in the ordinary way. The second one uses 31 March 1982 value.

In both computations, base indexation allowance on the higher of cost and 31 March 1982 value.

The final result is the lower gain, the lower loss or, if there is one gain and one loss, zero.

The 31 March 1982 value could only be used in place of cost from *6 April 1988* onwards.

A taxpayer can make an *election* to use only the 31 March 1982 value for all assets owned on that date.

Special disposals

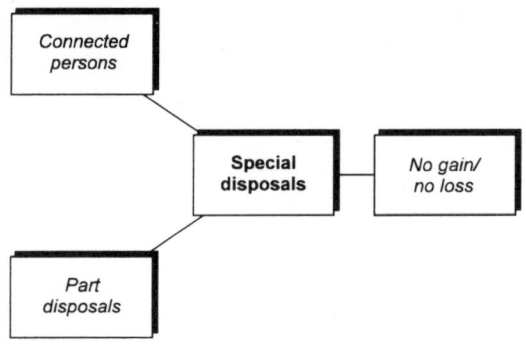

Connected persons

Disposals between connected persons are deemed to be for the market values of the assets (except where the no gain/no loss rule applies).

An individual is connected with his spouse and with his and his spouse's relatives (brothers, sisters, ancestors and lineal descendants) and their spouses.

A company is connected with

- A person who controls it

- Other companies under common control

No gain/no loss   *11/98*

Disposals between spouses and between companies in a 75% group do not give rise to gains or losses. The position on a later disposal is as follows.

- If the first company bought the asset before 1 April 1982, then when the second owner sells it, assume that they bought it when the first owner did

- If the first company bought the asset after 31 March 1982, then when the second owner sells it, assume that they bought it at the time of the no gain/no loss transfer, for its cost plus indexation up to then

Part disposals

On a part disposal, you are only allowed to take part of the cost of the asset into account.

- Costs attributable solely to the part disposed of are taken into account in full

- For other costs, take into account A/(A + B) of the cost
  - A is the proceeds of the part sold
  - B is the market value of the part retained

On a small part disposal of land, you can deduct the proceeds from the cost of the remaining land instead of computing a gain.

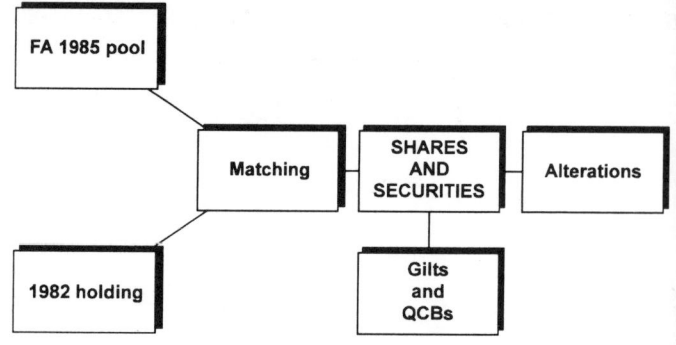

Matching

Shares of one class in one company are identical, but they may have been bought at different times for different prices. We therefore need matching rules to work out the cost of shares sold. Disposals by company shareholders are matched with acquisitions in the following order.

- Shares acquired on the same day

- Shares acquired in the previous nine days, taking earlier acquisitions first

- Shares from the FA 1985 pool

- Shares from the 1982 holding

- Shares acquired before 6 April 1965 (not examinable)

(Note: The matching rules for individual shareholders are different to the above.)

The FA 1985 pool   *5/95, 11/95, 5/96, 11/97, 5/98*

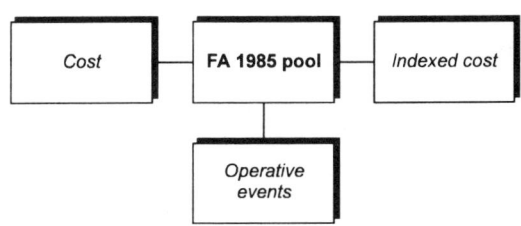

The FA 1985 pool includes shares acquired after 5 April 1982. It is kept in three columns, as follows.

- The *number of shares*

- The *cost*

- The *indexed cost*. This starts at 1 April 1985 for companies, with the cost of earlier acquisitions plus indexation to that date

  o At each *operative event*, increase it by the indexed rise since the last operative event, then add in the cost of shares acquired (or take out the indexed cost for shares disposed of)

  o The CIMA examiner will give you the indexed rise factors and a starting point for the pool

Operative events are acquisitions and disposals (apart from bonus issues).

- On an acquisition, add the cost to both the pool cost and the pool indexed cost

- On a disposal, take out a pro-rata slice of the cost and the indexed cost to use in the disposal computation

The indexation allowance is the indexed cost taken out of the pool minus the cost taken out.

The 1982 holding   5/95

This is a pool of shares acquired between 6 April 1965 31 March 1982 for companies inclusive.

- There are two columns, the number of shares and the cost

- On a disposal, take out a pro-rata slice of the cost to use in the disposal computation

    o Indexation allowance is worked out separately for each disposal, because it always runs from March 1982

Alterations   11/95, 11/96

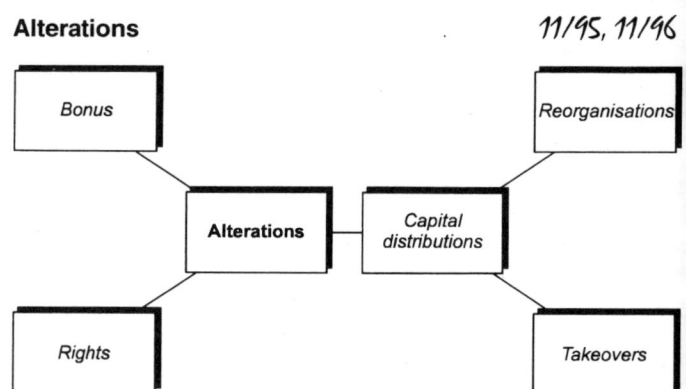

Bonus issues   11/97

Simply add the number of bonus shares received to the number of shares in the FA 1985 pool or the 1982 holding. Remember that bonus shares on 1982 holding shares go into that holding.

Rights issues   *11/98*

Treat rights taken up like any other purchase of shares, except that rights on 1982 holding shares go into that holding and their cost only gets indexation from the date of incurral, not from March 1982.

Treat a sale of rights like a capital distribution.

Capital distributions

Generally, treat a capital distribution as a part disposal.

However, if the proceeds do not exceed the higher of £3,000 and 5% of the value of the shares, you can deduct the proceeds from the cost of the shares instead.

Reorganisations and takeovers   *11/95, 5/98*

- Apportion the cost of the old shares to the new assets received in proportion to their values

- Where the new assets include cash, compute a chargeable gain using the cash received and the part of the cost of the old shares apportioned to that cash

> *Exam focus.* Questions which involve only one purchase of shares are common, but the examiner is likely to complicate them by putting a takeover between the purchase and the sale.

Gilts and qualifying corporate bonds (QCBs)

These are exempt assets for individuals.

For companies, profits and losses are revenue items and are dealt with under Schedule D Case I or Case III.

QCBs include most debentures acquired after 13 March 1984.

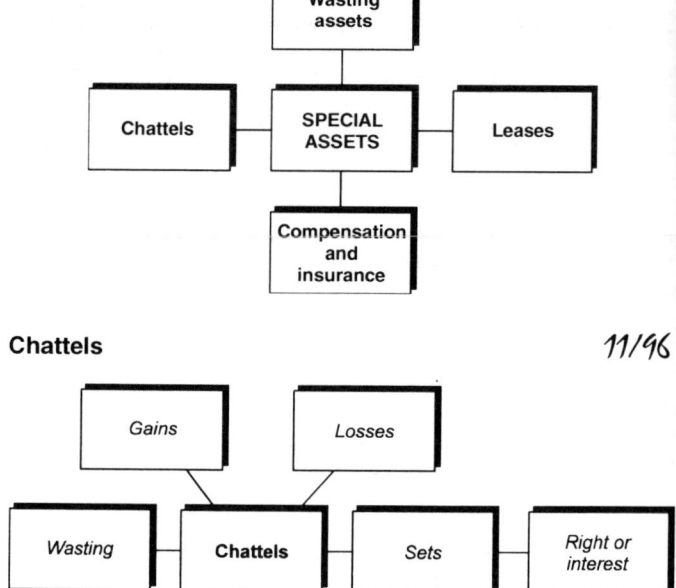

Chattels   *11/96*

A chattel is an item of tangible movable property.

- *Wasting chattels* are exempt from CGT, unless capital allowances could have been claimed on them

- *Gains* on chattels sold for gross proceeds of £6,000 or less are exempt. If proceeds exceed £6,000, the maximum gain is 5/3 of the excess

- *Losses* on chattels sold for gross proceeds of under £6,000 are restricted by assuming the proceeds to be £6,000

- If a *set* of chattels is broken up and sold as separate items to the same person or to persons connected with each other, the £6,000 rules are applied to the total of the sales

- If there is a part disposal of a chattel by selling a *right or interest*, the £6,000 limits are shared between the value of the part disposed of and the value of the part retained

Wasting assets

A wasting asset is one with an estimated remaining useful life of 50 years or less and whose original value will fall over time.

- Traded options do not have their cost written down over time
  - Non-traded options do have their cost written down over time, so no loss arises on their abandonment

- Other wasting assets have their cost written down over time. The write-down is straight-line except for leases
  - Assets eligible for capital allowances and used in a trade do not have their cost written down

Leases

11/96, 5/98

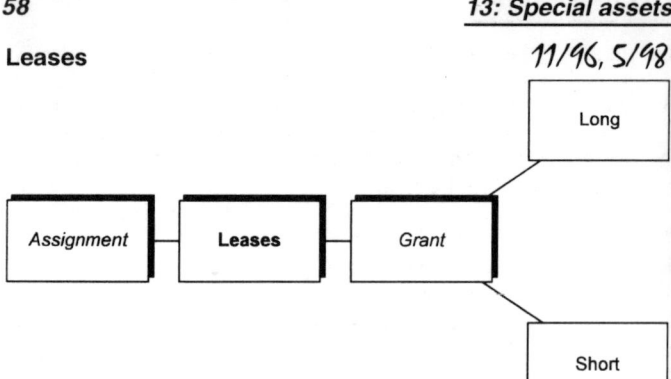

Assignment

- When a lease which still has at least 50 years to run is assigned, do an ordinary disposal computation

- On the assignment of a lease with less than 50 years to run, write down the cost using the table of percentages

  - Percentages must be worked out to the nearest month, taking 1/12 of the difference between two adjacent figures in the table for each month

  - In a computation based on 31 March 1982 value, we measure the life of the lease from that date

Grant: long

On a grant of a lease for 50 years or more, do an ordinary part disposal computation, using A/(A+B). A is the premium received, and B is the value of the rents plus the discounted value of the reversion.

- On a grant of a short lease out of a freehold or a long (50 years or more) lease, deduct the Schedule A element of the premium from the proceeds and from the top line of the part disposal fraction

- On a grant of a short lease out of a short lease
  - Use the table of percentages to find the part of the cost which covers the period of the lease granted
  - Deduct the Schedule A element of the premium from the gain at the end of the computation, but not so as to create a loss

Compensation and insurance

11/96

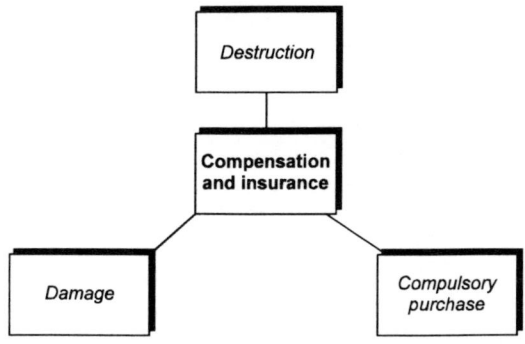

- When assets are *damaged*, compensation and insurance proceeds are treated as proceeds of a part disposal
  - However, if at least 95% of the proceeds for damage to a non-wasting asset are used to restore the asset or if the proceeds are small the proceeds may be deducted from the base cost of the asset instead

- A sum is small for this purpose if either it is less than 5% of the value of the asset or it is less than £3,000

  o If less than 95% of the proceeds are used for restoration, the part so used can be deducted from the base cost

- On the *destruction* of an asset, there is an ordinary disposal computation

  o However, if some or all of the proceeds for a non-wasting asset are used to replace the asset within 12 months, the gain minus the amount not so used can be deducted from the base cost of the replacement

- A *compulsory purchase* of land can be treated in the same way as the destruction of an asset, if replacement land is bought within one year before to three years after the disposal

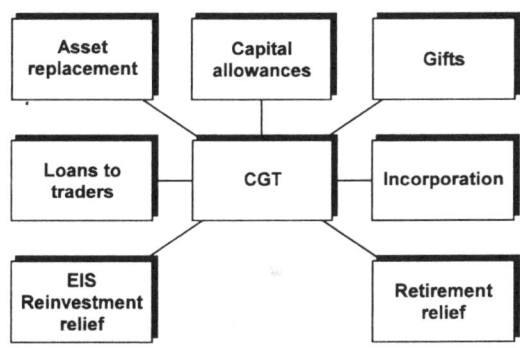

Many reliefs available to business are holdover reliefs which defer gains by deducting the gain from the cost of an asset, so that the gain on a later disposal of the asset will be increased.

Asset replacement   *11/95, 5/96, 11/97, 11/98*

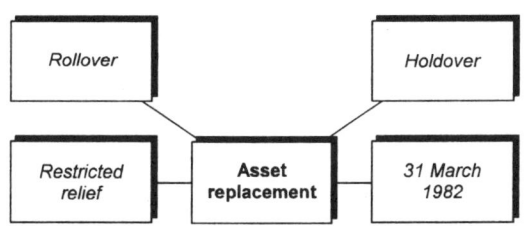

Individuals and companies can claim relief for gains on business assets being replaced if both the old and the new assets are on the list of eligible assets, and the new asset is bought between 12 months before and 36 months after the disposal.

Rollover

If the new asset is not depreciating, relief is given by deducting the gain from the cost of the new asset.

Holdover

If the new asset is depreciating, the gain is merely deferred. It becomes chargeable when the new asset is sold or ceases to be used for the purposes of the trade, or ten years after its acquisition, whichever occurs first.

If a non-depreciating qualifying asset is acquired before the gain becomes chargeable, the gain may be rolled over into that asset.

Exam focus. If a question mentions the sale of some business assets and the purchase of others, look out for rollover or holdover relief but do not just assume that it is available: the assets might be of the wrong type, for example movable plant and machinery.

---

31 March 1982

If someone bought an old asset before 31 March 1982 and sold it before 6 April 1988, rolling over a gain into a new asset bought after 31 March 1982, apply a special rule: on the sale of the new asset, only deduct half of the rolled over gain from its cost.

Restricted relief

If part of the proceeds of the old asset are not reinvested, the gain is chargeable up to the amount not reinvested.

Relief is proportionately restricted when an asset has not been used for trade purposes throughout its life (ignoring periods before 1 April 1982).

Capital allowances

When capital allowances have been obtained on any asset, and there would be an allowable loss, the cost must be reduced by the lower of the loss and the net allowances. The normal result is to eliminate the loss.

Gifts 11/97

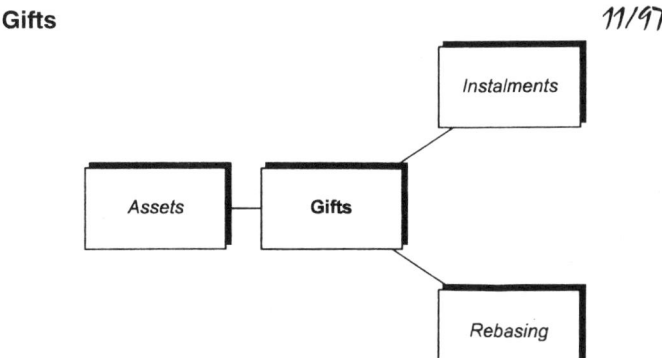

When gift relief is claimed, the gain on the gift or sale at undervalue is deducted from the recipient's base cost. If there are actual sale proceeds exceeding cost, the excess is deducted from the relievable gain.

Assets

Only certain assets qualify for gift relief. They are assets owned by an individual and used in a trade, and shares and securities in the donor's personal company.

> *Exam focus*. Never suggest claiming gift relief until you have decided whether the asset is of the right type.

Instalments

If gift relief is unavailable on land, controlling shareholdings or unquoted minority shareholdings, the CGT may be paid by ten annual instalments (with interest).

Rebasing

If gift relief was claimed on a disposal after 31 March 1982 and before 6 April 1988, and the donor acquired the asset before 31 March 1982, only half of the relief is deducted from the donee's base cost.

Incorporation   *5/95, 5/98*

A relief applies when a business is incorporated as a going concern, all its assets (or all except cash) are transferred to the company and the consideration is at least partly in shares.

Part of the gain is passed into the shares and deducted from their base cost, instead of being immediately chargeable. The proportion of the gain so dealt with is the proportion of the total consideration represented by the shares.

Retirement relief

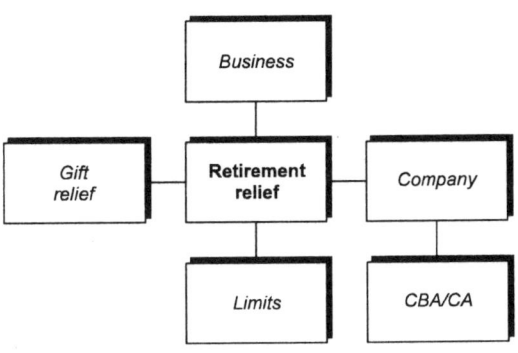

Retirement relief is available when the disposer is aged at least 50 or is retiring through ill health.

- It is given on the sale of a *business* or a part of a business

- It is also given on the sale of shares or securities in a personal *company*

  - The eligible gain is the full gain × *CBA/CA* (the company's chargeable business assets/its chargeable assets)

- The *limits* on retirement relief are the first £250,000 of the gain (full relief) and the next £750,000 (half relief)

  - These limits are scaled down on a time basis for qualifying periods of between one and ten years

- If *gift relief* is also available, retirement relief is given first

- Retirement relief is due to be phased out gradually from 6 April 1999 onwards

EIS Reinvestment relief (CGT deferral relief)   *11/96*

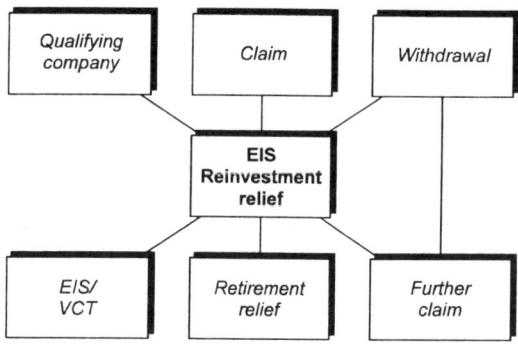

- EIS Reinvestment relief allows a gain on any asset to be deferred when ordinary shares in an EIS company are acquired between one year before and three years after the disposal

- A *qualifying company* is an unquoted company carrying on a qualifying trade which qualifies for EIS relief

- The gain is deferred and becomes chargeable only if the shares are sold or if certain conditions are not satisfied within a five year period

- A *claim* may be for any specified amount of the gain, up to the cost of the shares

- *Withdrawal* of relief follows the company's ceasing to qualify or the taxpayer's becoming neither resident nor ordinarily resident in the UK

  ○ A *further claim* using other shares may defer the gain

- If *retirement relief* and EIS reinvestment relief are claimed on the same disposal, the claim for EIS reinvestment relief should be adjusted to take account of the retirement relief

- *VCT* shares may also be used

Loans to traders

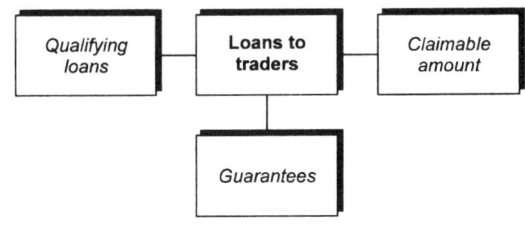

Relief can be claimed for losses on qualifying loans (individuals only) or on guarantees of loans (individuals and companies).

- A *qualifying loan* is a loan used for trade purposes which is not a debt on a security, or which is a qualifying corporate bond

- The *claimable amount* is the irrecoverable capital. Lost interest cannot be claimed

- For a payment under a *guarantee*, the amount paid can be claimed, whether it is in respect of capital or interest

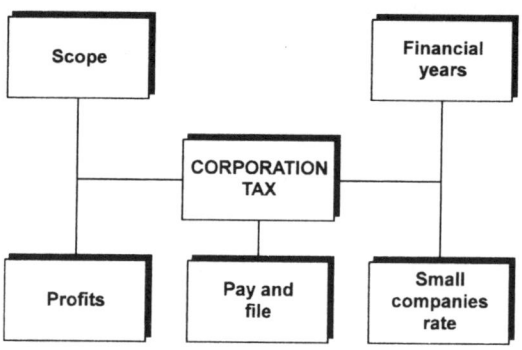

Scope

Corporation tax is charged on the worldwide profits of UK resident companies, and on the profits of a UK branch or agency of a non-UK resident company.

Tax is charged for accounting periods. An accounting period can never exceed 12 months.

If a period of account exceeds 12 months, the first 12 months form the first accounting period in it. Profits are divided between accounting periods as follows.

- Trading income: time-apportion the amount before capital allowances, then compute capital allowances separately for each period

- Rental income: allocated to the period in which it is due to be received

- Other income, gains and charges: allocate to the period to which they relate, except for Schedule D Case VI income, which is time-apportioned

Profits   5/95, 11/95, 5/96, 11/96, 5/97, 11/97, 5/98, 11/98

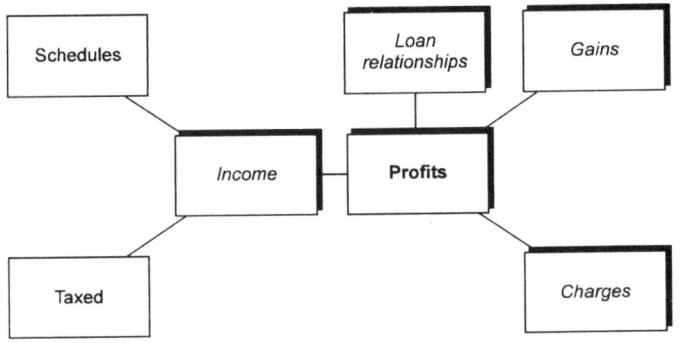

- *Income* is classified into the same *schedules* as apply for income tax purposes (but Schedule D Case I or Case III for all interest, UK or foreign, received gross or net)

- Schedule A income is computed in the same way as for individuals but losses are relieved in the same way as management expenses of investment companies

- *Taxed income* comes into the computation gross

- Bank and building society interest is received gross

- Dividends from other UK companies are not taxable income

- *Loan relationships* for trading purposes give rise to Schedule D Case I income or expenses. Non-trading relationships give rise to Schedule D Case III income or a non-trading deficit

> _Exam focus._ A recent recurring theme in the Paper 12 exam is the loan relationship rules being built into the compulsory CT question in a minor way and then also examined as a separate question in Section C of the exam.

- Chargeable _gains_ are included in profits

- _Charges_ come off profits to arrive at profits chargeable to corporation tax. The gross amount of a charge is deducted

> _Exam focus._ Although the schedules and the adjustment of trading profit are the same as for income tax, the similarity stops there: _never_ apply basis period rules, tax years or income tax rates to a company.

Financial years

Rates of tax are set for financial years. FY 1998 runs from 1 April 1998 to 31 March 1999.

If an accounting period straddles a change in rates, the results of the period are simply time-apportioned to the two financial years.

The small companies rate   _5/95, 11/95, 11/96, 5/97, 5/98_

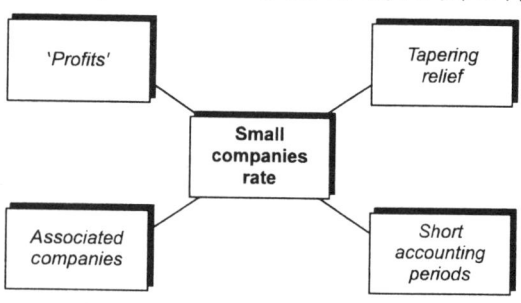

The small companies rate applies if a company's *'profits'* are below the lower limit. 'Profits' are profits chargeable to corporation tax, plus dividends (including tax credits) received from outside the group.

Tapering relief is given if 'profits' fall between the limits.

The limits are multiplied by months/12 for *short accounting periods* and are shared equally between *associated companies*.

Pay and file

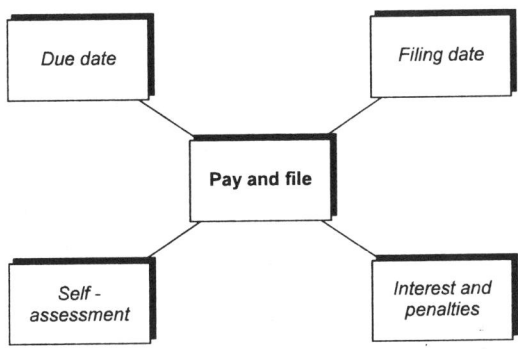

- The *due date* for corporation tax is nine months and a day after the last day of the accounting period

- The *filing date* is 12 months after the last day of the accounting period

  o A return form CT 200 must be submitted by this date

  o Later changes to claims can be made on form CT 201 or by letter

- *Interest* runs from the due date. Overpaid tax earns interest from the later of that date and the date it is paid

- *Penalties* for late submission of a return start with a £100 fixed penalty, rising to £200 after a delay of three months. For delays of over 6 months and up to 12 months, there is an additional penalty of 10% of the tax still unpaid six months after the filing date. For a delay of over 12 months the penalty is 20% of that tax

- Under the new system of *self-assessment* for companies, a company's return form will include an assessment prepared by the company itself. This system does not apply to accounting periods ending before 1.7.99.

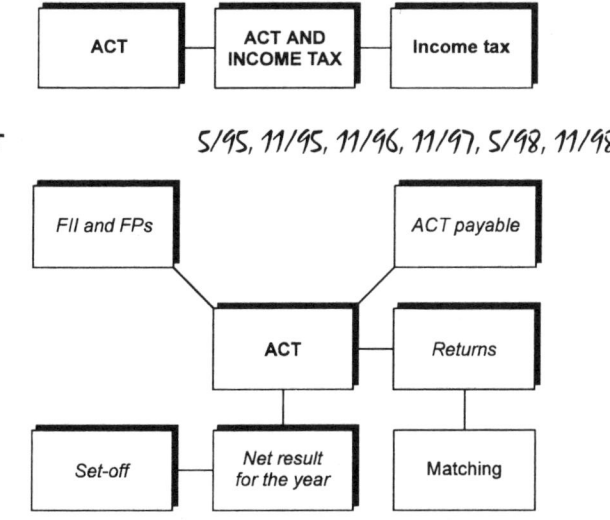

FII and FPs

When a company receives dividends from another UK company, the income, grossed up at the ACT rate (net × 100/80), is *FII* (franked investment income).

Dividends from overseas are not FII. They are income taxable under Schedule D Case V

Dividends received under a group income election are not FII

When a company pays a dividend, the payment, grossed up at the ACT rate, is an *FP* (franked payment).

Dividends paid under a group income election are not FPs

The *ACT payable* is (FPs − FII) × the ACT rate as a percentage of gross amounts (20%).

Returns

- ACT returns are made *quarterly*, for periods ending on 31 March, 30 June, 30 September and 31 December, and also for the period to the end of an accounting period

---

Exam focus. Always prepare returns in gross terms (FII and FPs).

- The *matching* of *FII* and *FPs* takes place on each return and the ACT or the FII carried forward is then found
  - FII may also be carried back within the same accounting period, to obtain a repayment of ACT

- The *net result for the year* must be computed
  - The *current year set-off* of ACT paid is limited to the taxable profits × 20%
  - *Surplus ACT* may be carried back, carried forward or surrendered to subsidiaries
  - Surplus FII is carried forward against future FPs

- ACT will be abolished from 6 April 1999. Arrangements will exist to utilise surplus ACT at this date

Income tax *5/95, 11/96, 11/97, 5/98*

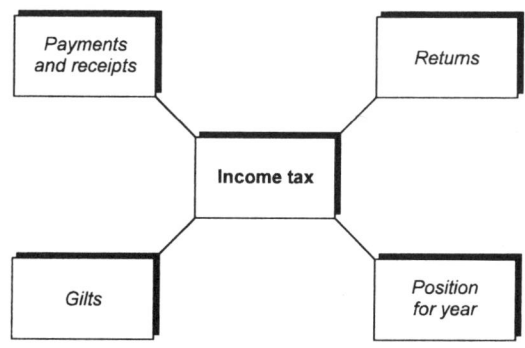

The system for income tax ensures that deducting income tax from *payments* and *receipts* has no net effect on companies.

● Income tax withheld from payments must be paid over

● Income tax suffered on receipts is reclaimed

Returns are made for the same periods as ACT returns.

Exam focus. Always prepare returns in terms of tax deducted and suffered. Remember that the tax rate is 20% for interest, but 23% (FY 98) for charges paid or received.

The *position for the year* must be worked out at the end of the year. There is always a full set-off of any income tax suffered against corporation tax. No amounts are carried forward.

Companies could elect prior to 6 April 1998 to receive interest on *gilts* gross, but must then account for 20% income tax quarterly. From 6 April 1998 all gilt interest will be paid gross.

Trading losses

A trading loss incurred by a company may be:

- set off against current period profits (before charges are deducted) and then;

- set off against the profits (after trade charges but not non-trade charges are relieved) of the previous 12 months

- Alternatively a trading loss may be carried forward for offset against the first available Sch D Case I profits of the same trade. Unrelieved trade charges can also be offset in this way

- The 12 month carry back period is extended to 36 months where the trading loss arose in the 12 months prior to a cessation of trade. Any unrelieved trade charges can also be added to the loss carried back when a company ceases to trade

- Non-trading deficits on loan relationships can be relieved in the same way as trading losses but a carry back claim is for offset against Sch D Case III profit on loan relationships only

- Capital losses can only be set against capital gains (never income) in the current and future accounting periods

- No relief is available for trading losses in accounting periods on one side of a change in ownership (CIO) of a company against profits on the other side if:
  - there is a major change in the nature or conduct of the trade within 3 years of the CIO (either side)
  - after the CIO there is a considerable revival of the trading activities

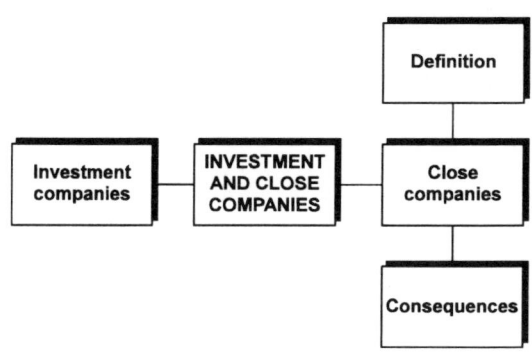

Investment companies

An investment company is a company whose business is to make investments.

- *Management expenses* are deductible in computing taxable profits. Unrelieved management expenses may be carried forward and treated as expenses of the next accounting period. The carry-forward goes on for as many periods as necessary, until the expenses are relieved

Close companies: definition   11/95, 5/97

A close company is a company which is under the control of five or fewer participators (broadly, shareholders), or of any number of participator-directors.

- Treat the shareholdings of associates of participators as if they were held by the participators

- Control is given by having more than half of the shares, the votes, the income (assuming it is all distributed) or the assets on a winding up

- Quoted companies are not close if

   o At least 35% of the votes are held by the public, and

   o The principal members (the top five) do not have more than 85% of the votes

Close companies: consequences   *11/95*

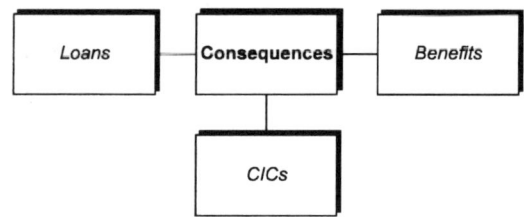

- If a close company makes a *loan* to a participator, it must pay notional ACT to the Revenue

   o This notional ACT is only repayable when the loan is repaid

   o If an amount is written off, treat this as a net dividend for the participator and no tax repayment for the company

- If a participator gets a *benefit* in kind not taxed under Schedule E, treat the Schedule E value as a dividend. Disallow the actual cost in adjusting the company's profits

- A *CIC* (close investment-holding company) always pays the full rate (31% FY 1998) of corporation tax

   o Repayments of tax credits on dividends paid by CICs may be restricted

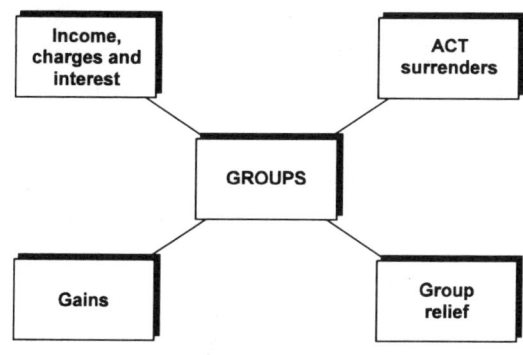

Exam focus. When dealing with groups, always establish the percentage holding at each level and the effective interest of the holding company in each subsidiary. These figures will determine the reliefs available.

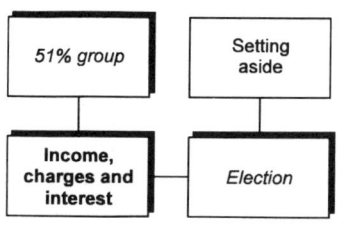

Income   5/95, 11/95, 5/96, 11/97, 5/98

Dividends can be paid within a *51% group* as *group income.*

- An *election* must be made in advance

- There is no ACT on a dividend paid as group income. It is not a franked payment, and it is not FII of the recipient

- An election may be *set aside* to pay a dividend outside it
  - This can be used to pass FII received by the subsidiary up to the parent company

Charges and interest

Charges and interest can be paid within a *51% group* without deducting income tax. An *election* must be made in advance.

ACT surrenders   *5/97, 5/98*

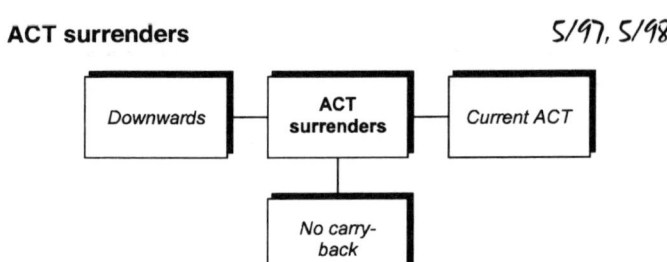

ACT can be surrendered *downwards* within a 51% group. Only *current* ACT (whether or not surplus) can be surrendered, not ACT brought forward. *No carry-back* of surrendered ACT by the recipient is allowed.

Group relief   *5/95, 5/96, 11/96, 11/97, 5/98, 11/98*

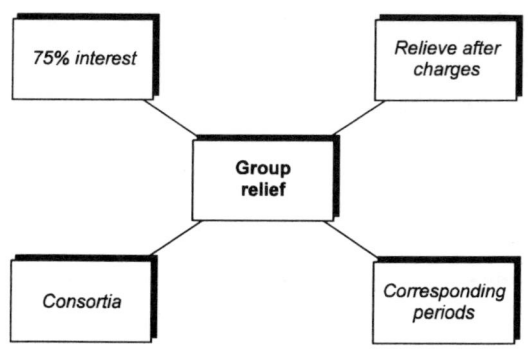

Group relief allows trading losses of one group company to be set against total profits of another.

> *Exam focus.* Give group relief where it will save most tax: firstly to companies in the tapering relief band (marginal rate 33.5%), then to companies paying the full 31% rate and finally to companies paying the small companies rate.

75% interest

One company must have a 75% effective interest in the other, or there must be a third company which has a 75% effective interest in both.

Relieve after charges

Group relief is set against total profits after charges.

Corresponding accounting periods

Group relief is strictly a current period relief. If accounting periods do not coincide, the profits and losses must be time-apportioned. Only the profits and losses of the period of overlap may be matched up.

Consortia

If a company is 75% owned by other companies, each owning at least 5%, losses can be surrendered by that company to the consortium members or vice versa.

The maximum surrender to or from any one member is that member's percentage stake × the owned company's profit or loss.

Gains   *5/95, 5/96, 5/97, 5/98, 11/98*

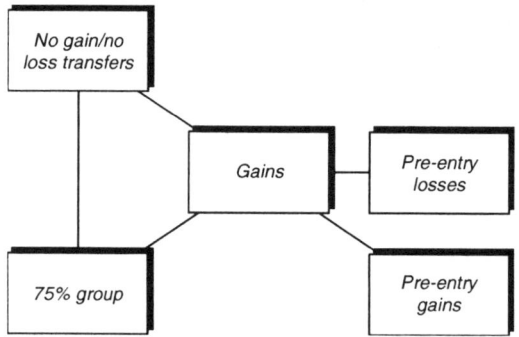

No gain/no loss transfers

There are no gain/no loss transfers when assets are transferred within a *75% group*.

A 75% group starts with the top company (which must always be included). It carries on down so long as there is a 75% holding at each level and the effective interest of the top company is over 50%.

Pre-entry losses 5/98

If a company with capital losses joins a group, those losses cannot be set against gains on assets which are then acquired from within the group.

If the company comes into the group owning assets which it then disposes of at a loss, use of the pre-entry proportion of the loss is restricted in the same way.

Pre-entry gains

Capital gains which have been realised before a company joins a group must be identified and group capital losses cannot be offset against such gains.

Reorganisations

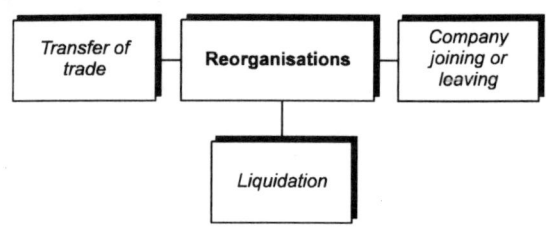

Transfer of trade

If a trade is transferred with no real change of ownership, trading losses may be carried forward. Capital allowances computations also continue undisturbed.

On a transfer for no consideration other than the assumption of liabilities, assets can be transferred at no gain and no loss.

Company joining or leaving a group

When a company joins a group, the number of associated companies increases and the tax privileges available to groups become available to the new member.

These consequences reverse when a company leaves a group. In addition, if the leaver received assets from other group members at no gain and no loss within the previous six years, chargeable gains may arise on those assets.

Liquidation

Accounting periods will end on each of the cessation of trade, the resolution for winding up and the end of winding up.

The main tax problem on a liquidation is often the use of losses. Final period trading losses can only be set against gains on the disposal of assets if the assets are sold before trading ceases. A loss to be carried back from the final period can be augmented by unrelieved trade charges.

Planning

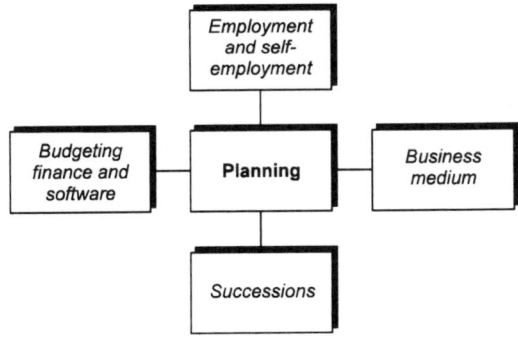

Employment and self employment

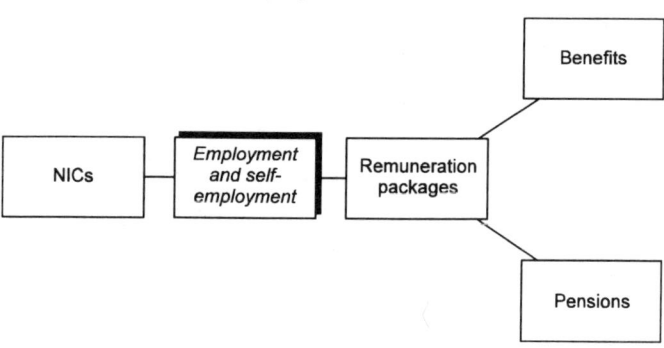

Someone may be able to choose between being employed and being self-employed. The main goal of tax planning is to minimise the total amount taken by the government, over the whole life of the business and in retirement.

- *NICs* are generally a much heavier burden on the employed than on the self-employed, but on the other hand only people who have been employed can claim certain state benefits

- *Remuneration packages* for employees should be carefully planned

  - Some *benefits* give rise to deemed income which is less than the true worth of the benefit

- *Pensions* are a valuable benefit, with contributions by the employer not being taxable, contributions by the employee being deductible and the fund growing tax-free

Business medium *11/97, 5/98*

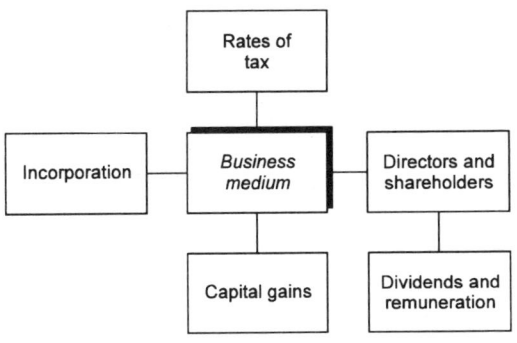

A trader must choose between trading as a sole trader and trading through a company. The points made above about employment (probably as a director) versus self-employment are of course relevant.

- *Rates of tax:* a small company pays tax at 21%, whereas a sole trader making only very modest profits pays tax at 40%. Income tax rates will apply to profits extracted from a company as remuneration or dividends

- *Directors and shareholders:* in a small incorporated business, the shareholders and the directors will often be the same people. This allows a choice between *dividends and remuneration*

  o *Dividends* do not give rise to NICs

  o *Remuneration* does give rise to NICs, but (up to the earnings cap) it counts as net relevant earnings for personal pension purposes

- *Capital gains:* if a sole trader makes a gain on an asset, it is taxed once. If, on the other hand, a company makes a gain, not only is it subject to corporation tax, but the gain when the shareholders dispose of their shares is also increased by the increase in the value of the company

- *Incorporation* has several tax consequences   *5/98*

  o It affects the final year's profits subject to income tax

  o It leads to disposals of assets for CGT purposes. However, if all of a business's assets (or all except cash) are transferred in exchange for shares, the chargeable gains are deducted from the base cost of the shares

  o The transfer of a business as a going concern is outside the scope of VAT, and the company may take over the VAT registration

---

Exam focus. When a question is about incorporation, stop and check the detailed information given: which reliefs do the facts hint at, and are those reliefs really available?

Successions to businesses

When someone sells or gives away their unincorporated business or shares in their private company, you need to consider the following points.

- There is likely to be a *gain* on sale

  o CGT *reliefs* (retirement and gift) may help

- If the disposal is to a connected person, an election to avoid balancing charges in capital allowances computations may be appropriate

- In the case of a company it may be sensible to extract some wealth as dividends prior to the disposal

- In the case of an unincorporated business, the basis period rules could result in a large tax charge in the final year

Budgeting

Most companies have to control cash flows carefully, including payments of tax. Payments can be delayed by the following methods.

- Using loss reliefs efficiently

- Using group income and group charges elections

- Delaying dividends into the next quarterly return period, or delaying asset disposals into the next accounting period

Finance

When planning a business's financial structure, the key distinction is between equity and debt. Only the cost of debt is tax-deductible, but all businesses need some equity.

Software

Computer software can help both in tax planning ('what if' calculations and analysis of tax law) and in preparing computations and returns.

| UK companies | OVERSEAS ASPECTS OF CORPORATION TAX | Double taxation relief |

UK companies

11/95, 5/97

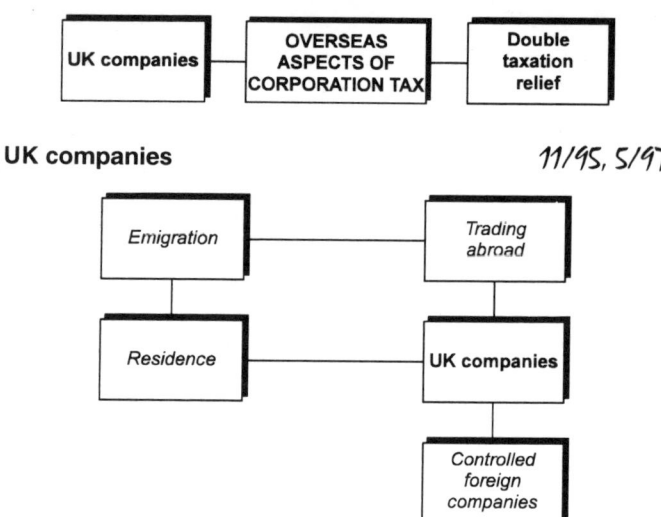

Residence

A company is resident in the UK if it is incorporated in the UK or if its central management and control are in the UK.

A UK resident company is subject to corporation tax on its worldwide profits. A non-UK resident company is only subject to corporation tax on the profits of a UK branch or agency.

Emigration

A company which ceases to be UK resident must pay an exit charge, based on a deemed disposal at market value of all its assets not retained in a UK branch or agency.

Trading abroad

- Overseas profits may be taxable under Schedule D Cases I, III or V, or as chargeable gains

- An overseas operation may be a branch or a subsidiary

  o A subsidiary's profits will only be taxable in the UK if they are passed to the parent (for example as dividends) or if the controlled foreign companies rules apply

Controlled foreign companies (CFCs)   *11/95, 11/97*

- A CFC is a company resident in a country with a tax rate of less than ¾ of the UK rate, which is controlled from the UK

- The profits of a CFC may be apportioned to UK companies with at least a 10% stake (rising to 25% for accounting periods ending after 30 June 1999) in the CFC, and subjected to UK tax (with credit for the overseas tax suffered)

- There are exemptions, including one for CFCs which distribute at least 90% of their profits and one for exempt activities

Double taxation relief (DTR)   5/95, 5/96, 5/97, 11/98

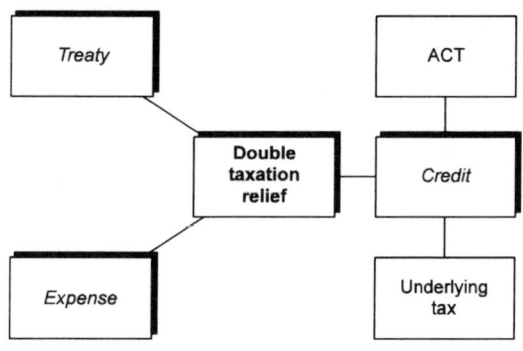

Treaty relief: relief may be given under a treaty between the two countries.

Credit relief: overseas profits may be brought into the computation gross, and relief for foreign tax deducted from the corporation tax.

- The relief is the lower of the foreign tax and the corporation tax (at the average rate) on the profits. Charges go against any profits the company chooses

- DTR is given before *ACT* is set off. ACT must be set against the corporation tax on each source of profits separately, computing a set-off limit for each source.

Underlying tax relief is available when the UK company holds at least 10% of the voting rights in the overseas company. It gives credit for foreign corporation tax.

Exam focus. Practise using a standard format for DTR computations, with columns (or rows) for corporation tax, DTR and ACT and rows (or columns) for the different sources of profits.

Expense relief

This is used when there is not enough corporation tax to set DTR against. The overseas profits are simply brought into the corporation tax computation net of the foreign tax.

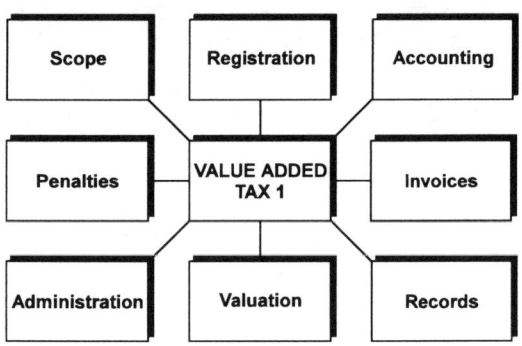

VAT is a tax on turnover, not on profits. It is imposed at each stage in a chain of sales, in such a way that the burden falls on the final consumer.

Exam focus. The examiner favours VAT questions requiring advice to new traders (should they register, etc) or to companies about to start trading abroad.

Scope

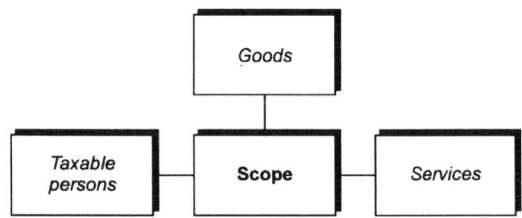

- VAT applies to taxable supplies of *goods* and *services* in the UK by a *taxable person*

- o A *taxable person* is someone who is registered for VAT, or ought to be registered

- VAT also applies to imports of *goods* from outside the European Community by any person. There are special rules for trade within the EC

Registration

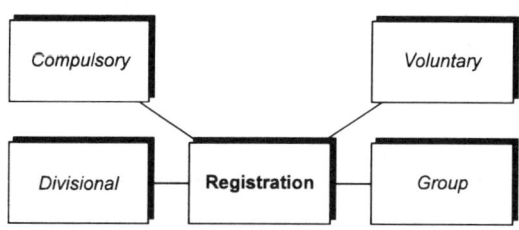

Compulsory registration

A trader must register for VAT if his taxable turnover (excluding VAT) has exceeded the registration limit in a past period not exceeding 12 months, or if there are reasonable grounds for believing that his taxable turnover for the next 30 days will exceed the registration limit.

Voluntary registration

A trader making taxable supplies may choose to register even though he does not have to.

Group registration   11/96

Companies under common control may choose group registration. Supplies between members of the VAT group are ignored for VAT purposes, and all transactions with third parties are treated as carried out by the representative member.

Divisional registration

A company may register its divisions separately. Supplies between the divisions are ignored.

Accounting   5/96

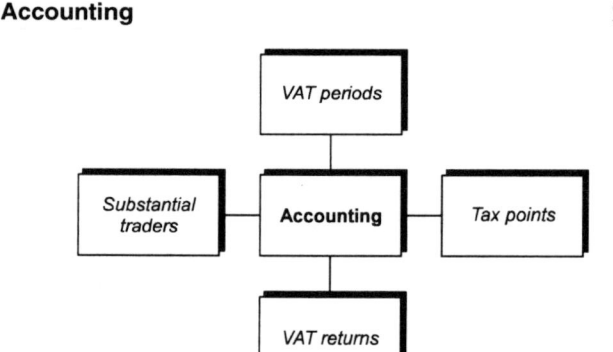

- A trader accounts for VAT for each *VAT period*. Periods are normally three months long, but they may last for one month or 12 months

- Each supply is treated as taking place on the *tax point*. In practice, this is usually the date of the invoice

- A *VAT return* is completed for each period. It shows the output VAT on sales, the input VAT on purchases and the VAT to be paid or reclaimed

- *Substantial traders* (those with VAT liabilities of over £2,000,000 a year) with three-month periods must make monthly payments on account of their VAT liabilities

Invoices

The required *contents* of a VAT invoice include the name, address and VAT number of the supplier, the name and address of the customer, a description of the supply and the amount and rate of VAT.

Retailers can issue *less detailed* invoices for supplies worth up to £100 including VAT.

Records

- *Source documents* which must be kept include invoices and credit notes received, copies of invoices and credit notes issued and documents relating to imports and exports

- *Summaries* which must be kept include summaries of supplies made and received and a VAT account

Valuation

- Sales are generally valued at the price paid

- A *mixed supply* is split into components, and the appropriate VAT rate is applied to each component

- A *composite supply* is not split, but is subjected to one VAT rate

- Where a *discount* for prompt payment is offered, VAT is computed on the price after deducting the discount, even if the discount is not taken up

Administration

- Local VAT offices carry out general administration, advise traders and check that the law is being properly applied

- VAT returns and payments go to the VAT Central Unit at Southend

- If HM Customs & Excise are not satisfied with the figures supplied by a trader, they can issue assessments for the VAT which they believe to be due

- Most decisions by HM Customs & Excise can be appealed against. Appeals are heard by VAT and duties tribunals. Further appeals go to the courts

Penalties

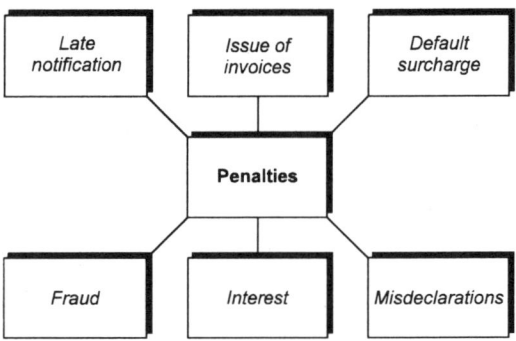

- *Late notification* of liability to register leads to a penalty of 5%, 10% or 15% of the VAT due

- The penalty for the *unauthorised issue of tax invoices* is 15% of the VAT shown on them

- The *default surcharge* is imposed when VAT is paid late during a surcharge period. It rises for successive defaults from 2% to 15% of the VAT paid late

- *Misdeclarations* are penalised if they are very large or repeated. The penalty is 15% of the VAT which would have been lost

- *Interest* is charged on VAT which was or could have been assessed. It runs from when the VAT should have been paid to when it is paid but this period cannot exceed 3 years

- *Criminal fraud* can lead to a fine and imprisonment. *Civil fraud* can lead to a penalty of 100% of the VAT involved

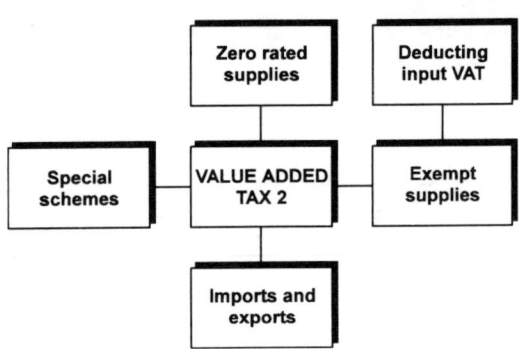

Zero rated supplies

Some supplies bear VAT, but at 0%. These are taxable supplies, so traders making them can recover input VAT. For example, a bookshop which buys a computer to use in the business could recover the VAT on it.

Zero rated supplies include food, books and newspapers, housebuilding and most exports.

Exempt supplies   *11/97*

Some supplies are exempt from VAT. They are not taxable, and traders making them cannot recover input VAT.

Exempt supplies include sales of land and buildings (other than by the builder), financial services, insurance, education and health services.

Deducting input VAT
11/97

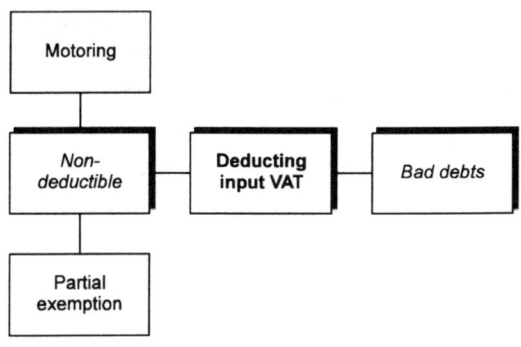

Non-deductible input VAT

- *Motoring:* input VAT on a car cannot be deducted unless the car has no non-business use, it is bought new for resale or it is for use in or leasing to a taxi business, a self-drive car hire business or a driving school

  - When a car is hired, the supplier deducted input VAT on its purchase and there is private use, the hirer can only deduct 50% of the VAT on the hire charge

- *Partial exemption:* if a trader makes some exempt supplies and some taxable supplies, the input VAT on purchases for exempt supplies cannot be deducted. Only a proportion of the input VAT which cannot be attributed to particular types of supply can be deducted

  - If input VAT attributable to or apportioned to exempt supplies does not exceed £625 a month on average and does not exceed 50% of all input VAT, all input VAT is deductible

---

Exam focus. You might have to advise a company which is
starting to make exempt supplies. Remember that although the
company may suffer a VAT cost, it will get corporation tax relief
on this cost: with a 31% corporation tax rate, £1,000 lost VAT
would only really cost £690.

Bad debts

If a debt is written off as bad and six months have passed
since the payment was due, the VAT element previously
accounted for and thus paid over to Customs can be
recovered. The supplier must notify the debtor of the claim
within 7 days. The debtor must repay to Customs any VAT
reclaimed which has not been paid to the supplier and on
which the supplier has claimed bad debt relief.

Imports and exports   5/95, 5/96, 11/98

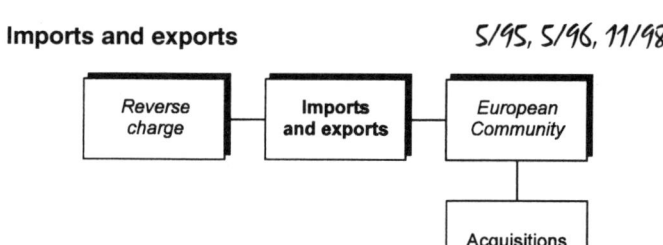

Imports of goods from outside the European Community (the
EC) are subject to VAT at the same rate as on a sale within
the UK. Exports of goods to outside the EC are zero rated.

The reverse charge

If services are supplied to a UK recipient from overseas, the recipient may be treated as making the supply. He will then have to account for VAT on the supply.

The European Community

- When goods are brought into the UK from within the EC, VAT is only due if there is a *taxable acquisition*. This is an acquisition of taxable goods by a taxable person for business purposes

- When a taxable person supplies goods within the EC, the supply is zero rated if the buyer is VAT registered and his registration number is shown on the invoice

Special schemes

- The cash accounting scheme allows traders to put purchases and sales into the VAT periods in which cash is paid or received

- The annual accounting scheme allows traders to prepare one VAT return a year. Payments on account of the ultimate VAT liability are required

- The secondhand goods scheme allows traders to account for VAT on the margin they make on each item

- The flat rate scheme for farmers allows farmers to opt out of VAT registration and instead add 4% to the selling price of their produce. This is input VAT for the buyer, but the farmer keeps it for himself